LSAT®

PrepTest 76

Unlocked

Exclusive Data, Analysis & Explanations for the
October 2015 LSAT

KAPLAN

PUBLISHING

New York

© 2017 by Kaplan, Inc.

Published by Kaplan Publishing, a division of Kaplan, Inc.
750 Third Avenue
New York, NY 10017

ISBN: 978-1-5062-2334-6
10 9 8 7 6 5 4 3 2 1

The Inside Story

PrepTest 76 was administered in October 2015. It challenged 33,229 test takers. What made this test so hard? Here's a breakdown of what Kaplan students who were surveyed after taking the official exam considered PrepTest 76's most difficult section.

Hardest PrepTest 76 Section as Reported by Test Takers

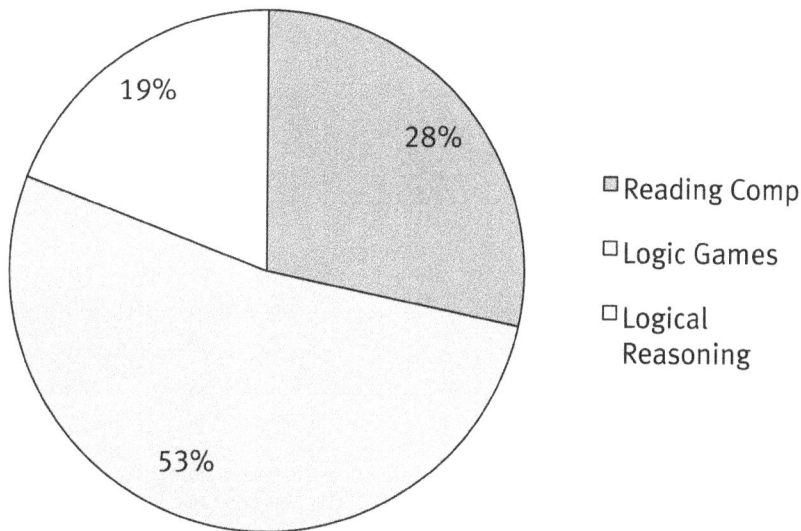

19%

28%

53%

- Reading Comp
- Logic Games
- Logical Reasoning

Based on these results, you might think that studying Logic Games is the key to LSAT success. Well, Logic Games is important, but test takers' perceptions don't tell the whole story. For that, you need to consider students' actual performance. The following chart shows the average number of students to miss each question in each of PrepTest 76's different sections.

Percentage Incorrect by PrepTest 76 Section Type

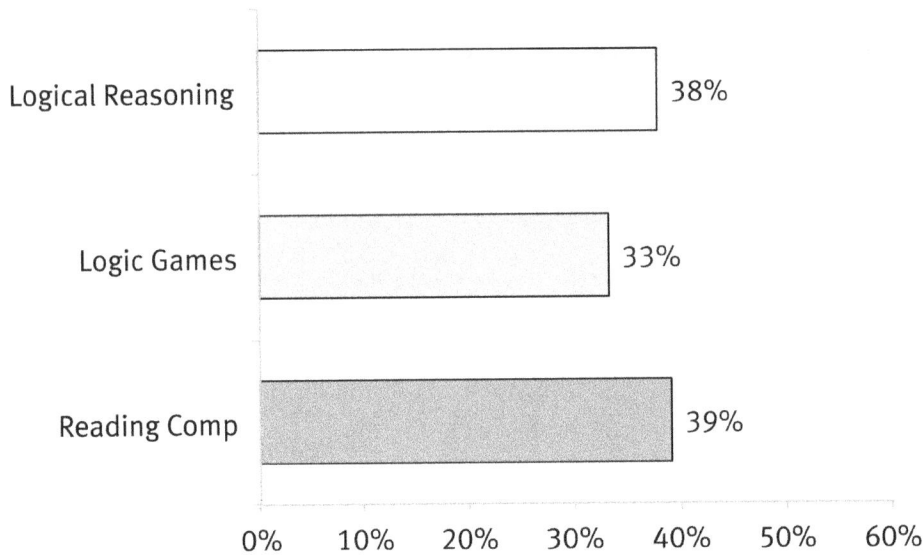

Logical Reasoning — 38%

Logic Games — 33%

Reading Comp — 39%

0% 10% 20% 30% 40% 50% 60%

Actual student performance tells quite a different story. On average, students were almost equally likely to miss questions in all three of the different section types, and on PrepTest 76, Reading Comprehension and Logical Reasoning were somewhat higher than Logic Games in actual difficulty.

Maybe students overestimate the difficulty of the Logic Games section because it's so unusual, or maybe it's because a really hard Logic Game is so easy to remember after the test. But the truth is that the test maker places hard questions throughout the test. Here were the locations of the 10 hardest (most missed) questions in the exam.

Location of 10 Most Difficult Questions in PrepTest 76

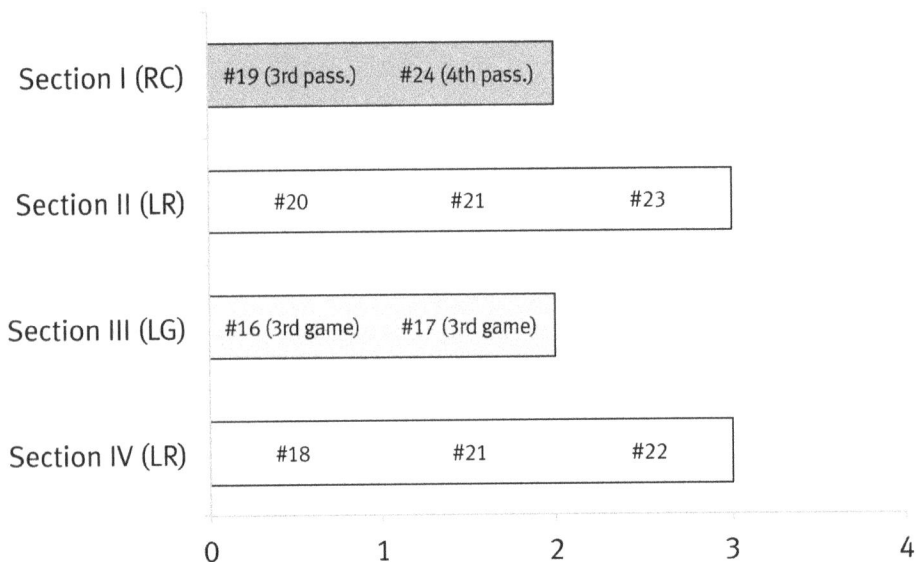

Section I (RC) — #19 (3rd pass.) #24 (4th pass.)

Section II (LR) — #20 #21 #23

Section III (LG) — #16 (3rd game) #17 (3rd game)

Section IV (LR) — #18 #21 #22

0 1 2 3 4

The takeaway from this data is that, to maximize your potential on the LSAT, you need to take a comprehensive approach. Test yourself rigorously, and review your performance on every section of the test. Kaplan's LSAT explanations provide the expertise and insight you need to fully understand your results. The explanations are written and edited by a team of LSAT experts, who have helped thousands of students improve their scores. Kaplan always provides data-driven analysis of the test, ranking the difficulty of every question based on actual student performance. The 10 hardest questions on every test are highlighted with a 4-star difficulty rating, the highest we give. The analysis breaks down the remaining questions into 1-, 2-, and 3-star ratings so that you can compare your performance to thousands of other test takers on all LSAC material.

Don't settle for wondering whether a question was really as hard as it seemed to you. Analyze the test with real data, and learn the secrets and strategies that help top scorers master the LSAT.

7 Can't–Miss Features of PrepTest 76

- With 12 Assumption questions, PrepTest 76 is tied for the most ever on a single LSAT. The only other time this happened was back in June of 2009 (PT 57).
- This was the first PrepTest since June '02 (PT 37) with no Main Point questions.
- PrepTest 76 featured two Strict Sequencing games—after only one on the three previous tests combined.
- In the second logic game—Newspaper Photographs—you'll want to check out a rarely used triple option setup.
- Answer choices (A) and (E) were never correct two times in a row, but choice (C) was correct three times in a row ... twice!
- PrepTest 76 was only the second LSAT (and first since December '09 (PT 59)) on which a Comparative Reading passage had eight questions.
- The second Comparative Reading passage discussed scientists calculating orbits. Maybe that was on the mind of test takers who had just seen *The Martian*, which was the #1 movie in America the week this test was administered.

PrepTest 76 in Context

As much fun as it is to find out what makes a PrepTest unique or noteworthy, it's even more important to know just how representative it is of other LSAT administrations (and, thus, how likely it is to be representative of the exam you will face on Test Day). The following charts compare the numbers of each kind of question and game on PrepTest 76 to the average numbers seen on all officially released LSATs administered over the past five years (from 2012 through 2016).

Number of LR Questions by Type: PrepTest 76 vs. 2012–2016 Average

PT 76 — 2012-2016 Average

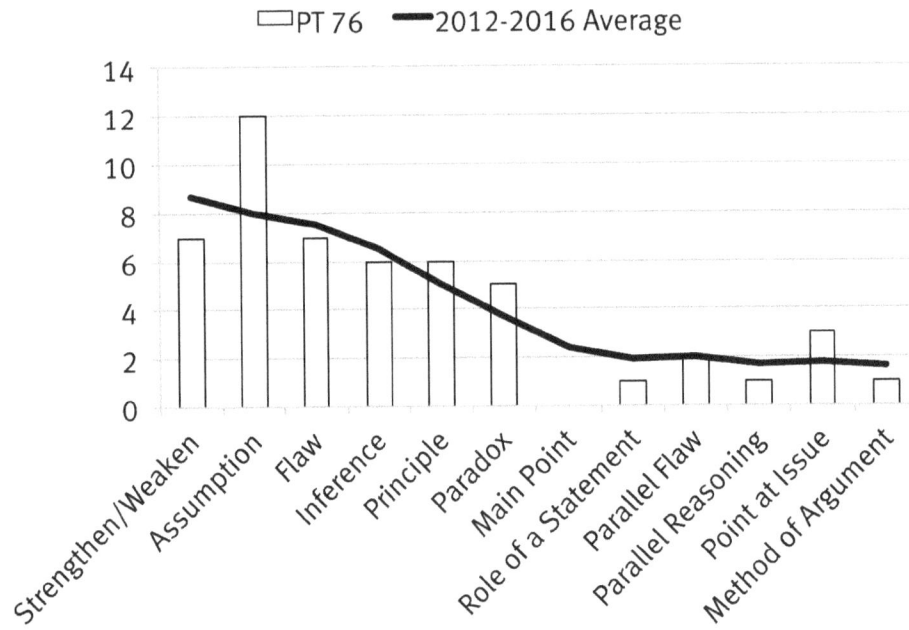

Number of LG Games by Type: PrepTest 76 vs. 2012–2016 Average

PT 76 — 2012-2016 Average

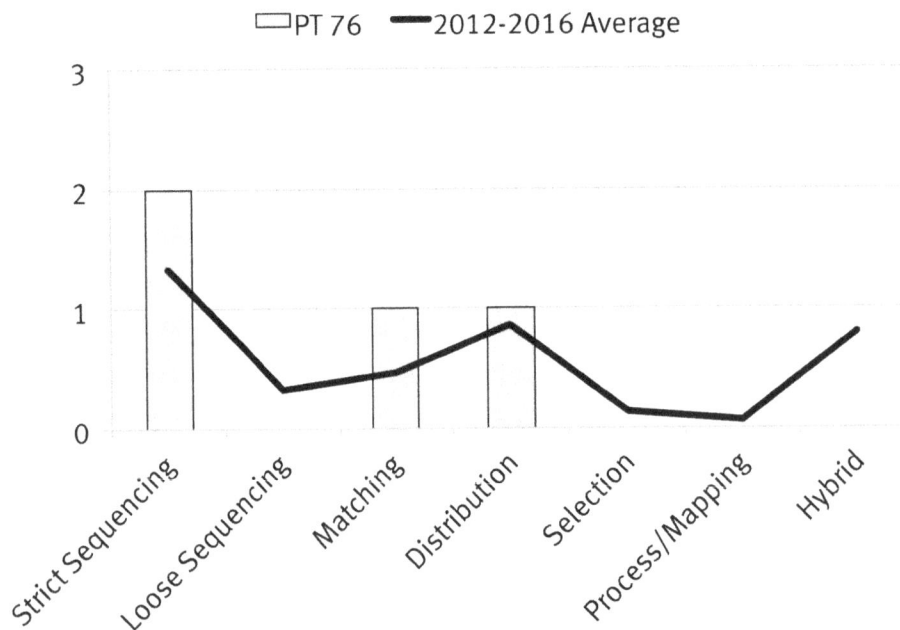

Number of RC Questions by Type: PrepTest 76 vs. 2012–2016 Average

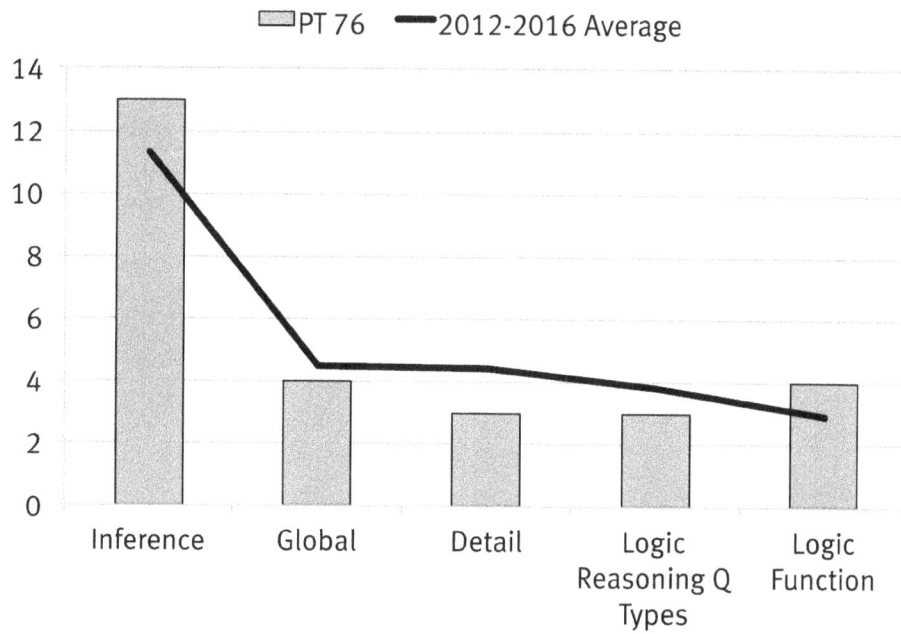

There isn't usually a huge difference in the distribution of questions from LSAT to LSAT, but if this test seems harder (or easier) to you than another you've taken, compare the number of questions of the types on which you, personally, are strongest and weakest. And then, explore within each section to see if your best or worst question types came earlier or later.

Students in Kaplan's comprehensive LSAT courses have access to every released LSAT and to an online Q-Bank with thousands of officially released questions, games, and passages. If you are studying on your own, you have to do a bit more work to identify your strengths and your areas of opportunity. Quantitative analysis (like that in the charts above) is an important tool for understanding how the test is constructed and how you are performing on it.

Section I: Reading Comprehension
Passage 1: Arnold Schoenberg

Q#	Question Type	Correct	Difficulty
1	Global	C	★
2	Logic Reasoning (Parallel Reasoning)	B	★
3	Logic Function	D	★★
4	Detail (EXCEPT)	A	★
5	Inference	D	★
6	Inference	A	★★★

Passage 2: Biotechnology Patents

Q#	Question Type	Correct	Difficulty
7	Global	D	★
8	Inference	B	★
9	Detail	B	★
10	Inference	C	★★
11	Logic Function	B	★
12	Inference	D	★★★
13	Inference	D	★★

Passage 3: Haudenosaune Wampum

Q#	Question Type	Correct	Difficulty
14	Global	B	★★
15	Logic Function	E	★
16	Logic Function	C	★★
17	Inference	C	★★
18	Inference	B	★★
19	Inference	E	★★★★

Passage 4: Negative Evidence in Science

Q#	Question Type	Correct	Difficulty
20	Global	C	★★★
21	Detail	C	★★
22	Inference	C	★★
23	Inference	D	★★★
24	Inference	B	★★★★
25	Logic Reasoning (Parallel Reasoning)	A	★★
26	Inference	B	★★
27	Logic Reasoning (Parallel Reasoning)	E	★★★

KAPLAN

Passage 1: Arnold Schoenberg

Step 1: Read the Passage Strategically

Sample Roadmap

line #	Keyword/phrase	¶ Margin notes
1–5		Quote—music sounds bad
8	But	NOT re: Schoenberg, but Beethoven
11	But	B & S controversy
12	controversy	B became popular
15	but	over time
17	significantly	
20	Like	B & S evolved
23	three	S—3 styles
28	ought to love	1) late-Romantic
34	Because … in his view … inevitable	2) atonal
35	he felt	
36	because	
37	compelled	
39	Finally	3) 12-tone
42	Awe-inspiring	Styles became more
44	more violent … therefore	difficult to follow
45	more difficult	
46	But	Auth:
47	but	Schoenberg's impact
51	essential	
54	disturbing … not because	
55	but because	

Discussion

The passage opens with a quote about some harsh-sounding music. Paragraph 2 suggests that this quote could easily apply to the music of Arnold Schoenberg, but it was actually about a piece by Beethoven.

Paragraph 3 describes how Schoenberg and Beethoven were both controversial, but mentions that Beethoven eventually became popular as people were able to listen to his music multiple times.

Paragraph 4 describes Schoenberg and Beethoven as innovators. At this point, the passage starts to concentrate primarily on Schoenberg's music, making him the **Topic**. This is also the start of a three-paragraph discussion of Schoenberg's three-stage stylistic evolution, which serves as the **Scope**. This paragraph mentions the first style: late-Romantic music.

Paragraph 5 introduces the second style: atonal music, which Schoenberg saw as a natural progression needed to express his ideas. Paragraph 6 brings up the third style: 12-tone music, which further refined atonal music. All three styles showed off Schoenberg's skills, but were also increasingly hard to listen to.

In paragraph 7, the author finally expresses a strong point of view: the style of music is not as important as the message the music conveys. This leads to a clearer understanding of the author's intentions. The **Purpose** is to evaluate the importance of Schoenberg's music. The author's praise of Schoenberg constitutes the **Main Idea**: Schoenberg's music was vital because it exposed listeners to emotions and truths never before heard in music.

1. (C) Global

Step 2: Identify the Question Type

This is a Global question because it asks for the "main point of the passage."

Step 3: Research the Relevant Text

Global questions are based on the entire text. Use the Main Idea as a perfect prediction here.

Step 4: Make a Prediction

Despite how some see Schoenberg's music as "shrill" and "difficult to follow," the author ultimately praises Schoenberg for his "awe-inspiring level of technical mastery" and his expression of "emotional states that music had not recorded before."

Step 5: Evaluate the Answer Choices

(C) correctly identifies the author's advocacy of Schoenberg's value in the face of critical reception.

(A) focuses too much on the negative reaction and not on the author's praise. And while the author would probably

encourage a wider appreciation for Schoenberg's music, the passage never confirms this has happened.

(B) is a Distortion. While Schoenberg and Beethoven share similarities, the author never suggests that they should be regarded as equals.

(D) is a 180. Line 49 directly states that Schoenberg was important "*not* because of the 12-tone system," but because of the message his music conveyed.

(E) is Out of Scope. The author never mentions how quickly, if at all, Schoenberg's music was accepted. This answer also fails to convey the author's appreciation for Schoenberg's music.

2. (B) Logic Reasoning (Parallel Reasoning)

Step 2: Identify the Question Type

The correct answer will be "analogous to" information provided in the passage. That makes this a Parallel Reasoning question.

Step 3: Research the Relevant Text

The word *disturbing* is in line 54, but the entire last sentence (lines 53–56) provides the relevant context.

Step 4: Make a Prediction

According to the last line, it is *not* the harshness of Schoenberg's music that makes it disturbing. What's disturbing is that it "unflinchingly faces difficult truths." The correct answer will describe another work that similarly addresses harsh realities.

Step 5: Evaluate the Answer Choices

(B) is a match. Difficult truths are exactly the kinds of things that "people would prefer to ignore."

(A) is Out of Scope. Vulgar language may be offensive, but it doesn't necessarily address "difficult truths."

(C) is Out of Scope. This would imply that Schoenberg was stealing from other composers, which is never mentioned or suggested.

(D) is Out of Scope. Political philosophies are never discussed. Furthermore, philosophies deal with personal beliefs rather than truths.

(E) is a Distortion. Saying a truth is unfamiliar doesn't mean it's difficult to face. In fact, people are probably *very* familiar with difficult truths and just don't want to listen to them.

3. (D) Logic Function

Step 2: Identify the Question Type

The phrase "in order to" indicates a Logic Function question. It's asking *why* the author included the opening quote.

Step 3: Research the Relevant Text

Beyond the quote itself, the second and third paragraph provide ample context for why the quote was included.

Step 4: Make a Prediction

According to the second paragraph, the quote describes a work by Beethoven. The third paragraph mentions how Beethoven is seen as an icon now, but he didn't develop that status until over a century after Kotzebue's remarks. So, the purpose here is to show—as the author later feels should apply to Schoenberg—that music initially deemed discordant could become appreciated over time.

Step 5: Evaluate the Answer Choices

(D) matches the contrast between early reaction and later reconsideration.

(A) is a Distortion. While the quote does refer to Beethoven's music, it is still one critic's opinion and not necessarily "accurate."

(B) mistakenly attributes the quote to a work of Schoenberg. While it resembles the reaction people have to Schoenberg's works, it's actually about the overture to Beethoven's *Fidelio*.

(C) takes one person's initial reaction and stretches it to a claim about all of Beethoven's works. However, Beethoven's works are now appreciated, and Beethoven is considered a cultural icon. The author also never suggests his works are uneven in quality.

(E) is Out of Scope. While critical consensus about Beethoven may have changed over the years, it is possible that Kotzebue's reaction was entirely consistent with other critics of his time.

4. (A) Detail (EXCEPT)

Step 2: Identify the Question Type

The question asks for what the author "alludes to," which may seem to indicate an Inference question. However, the answer choices here are lifted straight from the passage, making this a Detail question. Either way, four answers will come directly from the passage. The correct answer will not.

Step 3: Research the Relevant Text

The passage discusses both composers in the second, third, and fourth paragraphs.

Step 4: Make a Prediction

While impossible to predict what the correct answer will say, it helps to locate support for the wrong answers. They will all include similarities, which can be found by the Keywords [*b*]*oth* (line 11) and [*l*]*ike* (line 20). Expect an answer choice to point out an attribute of one composer that does not necessarily apply to the other.

Step 5: Evaluate the Answer Choices

(A) is correct because it only applies to Schoenberg (line 25). The passage never indicates the style in which Beethoven worked.

(B) is a similarity. These descriptors come directly from the quote about Beethoven's overture in the first paragraph. And the second paragraph states that this description also "characterizes the reaction of many listeners" to Schoenberg's music.

(C) is directly stated about both composers in lines 11–12.

(D) is mentioned in lines 20–21 about how both composers were alike.

(E) is an attribute of both composers mentioned in lines 12–13.

5. (D) Inference

Step 2: Identify the Question Type

The question asks for what the author "appear[s] to value." Because it merely appears as such (and thus isn't directly stated), this is an Inference question.

Step 3: Research the Relevant Text

The author's opinion is found primarily in the last paragraph.

Step 4: Make a Prediction

In lines 50–53, the author describes what makes Schoenberg's music *essential*: the inclusion of emotional aspects "music had not recorded before."

Step 5: Evaluate the Answer Choices

(D) is a perfect paraphrase of the *essential* quality of Schoenberg's work.

(A) is a Faulty Use of Detail. The technical mastery is described as *awe-inspiring* (line 42), but that doesn't make it more valuable than something *essential*. Lines 46–47 even say, "[b]ut the real issue for any piece of music is not how it is made, but what it has to say."

(B) is a Faulty Use of Detail. Shifting harmonies were just a part of Schoenberg's late-Romantic music (line 26). Nothing indicates that this was particularly valuable.

(C) is a 180. In line 49, the author states that the 12-tone system was *not* what made Schoenberg important.

(E) is a 180. In lines 46–47, the author suggests that the message is more important than the style. So the progression of styles wasn't important. What mattered is that he was able to say something through his music.

6. (A) Inference

Step 2: Identify the Question Type

The question asks for something *inferred* that the author is "most likely to agree with." That makes this an Inference question.

Step 3: Research the Relevant Text

The question asks about the relationship between Schoenberg's three styles, which are described in paragraphs 4–6.

Step 4: Make a Prediction

According to lines 32–33, Schoenberg took the first style of music (late-Romantic) and kept pushing it further and further until it transitioned into the second style (atonal). Schoenberg felt that second style was *inevitable*. Then, by lines 39–41, the third style (12-tone) took the second style and gave it order and stabilization. The correct answer will indicate this sense of purposeful transition.

Step 5: Evaluate the Answer Choices

(A) matches Schoenberg's intention of progress and development.

(B) is a 180. Schoenberg directly stated that the shift between the first two styles was an "inevitable step in the historical development of music." That makes it seem intentional, not *inexplicable* at all.

(C) is Half-Right, Half-Wrong. The progression between the first two styles was indeed *natural*, but so was the second progression. Schoenberg's goal in the third style was to bring order to the second style (lines 40–41).

(D) is Half-Right, Half-Wrong. The progression from the second to the third style was indeed *natural*, but so was the progression from the first to the second, which Schoenberg felt was *inevitable* (line 34). There were no *inexplicable* departures.

(E) is a 180 and a Distortion. The second style was not an *inexplicable* departure from the first—it was *inevitable* (line 34). Additionally, the third style built upon the second style, not the first one.

Passage 2: Biotechnology Patents

Step 1: Read the Passage Strategically

Sample Roadmap

line #	Keyword/phrase	¶ Margin notes
1	convinced	Biotech people
2	should	want protection
5	increasingly	But are
6	because	patents bad?
8	However	
9	hindering	
12	focus of increased scrutiny	
14	threat	Some patents restrict
20	fear	access to materials
23	In other instances	1) fear legal action
27	For example	2) patent holder
31	fear	wants exchange
35	While it is true	Auth:
37	also undoubtedly true	Arguments mistaken
41	seem to be confusing	1) legal action expensive
43	mistakenly assume	2) courts allow
47	questionable … First	noncommercial exceptions
51	Second	3) patents are good
54	Moreover	for innovation
55	spur rather than hinder … because	
56	compelling	

Discussion

Paragraph 1 opens with two biotechnology groups, each with a vested interest in protecting its intellectual property. Industries want to protect their commercial products, and academic institutions want to retain their funding. The Keyword [h]owever in line 8 is when the focus of the passage becomes clear. The **Topic** is biotechnology patents, and the **Scope** is the concerns scientists have about the effect of patents on basic research.

Paragraph 2 outlines the concerns. Researchers feel that patents prevent access to useful research material because either A) patent holders will sue anyone who tries to access that material, or B) patent holders will demand some sort of compensation in exchange for such access.

In paragraph 3, the author disputes these concerns (**Purpose**), suggesting that researchers are *confusing* the issue and *mistakenly* assuming that patents prevent basic research (**Main Idea**). For one thing, companies don't always take issues to court because it's expensive; they'll only sue if something threatens their place in the market system. Furthermore, courts tend to side with people who want to access material for noncommercial purposes. The author wraps up by pointing out the benefit of patents: They give scientists a "compelling incentive to innovate."

7. (D) Global

Step 2: Identify the Question Type

This is a Global question because it asks for the "main point of the passage."

Step 3: Research the Relevant Text

Because this is a Global question, the entire passage is relevant.

Step 4: Make a Prediction

The Main Idea from Step 1 provides an adequate prediction: researchers are mistaken in their belief that biotechnology patents are preventing them from performing basic research.

Step 5: Evaluate the Answer Choices

(D) is correct.

(A) is a 180. This is consistent with the opinions expressed in paragraph 2, but the author directly disputes this concern in paragraph 3.

(B) is too narrow. This expresses the conflict raised at the end of paragraph 1, but completely ignores the author's response in paragraph 3.

(C) is Out of Scope. The author says nothing about academics or industries being penalized. Furthermore, if anything the author thinks the current patent system is *fair* because he calls the concerns regarding perceived threats *questionable* (line 47).

(E) is too narrow, focusing on just one detail from paragraph 3 that supports the broader argument that patents are not as restrictive as some researchers believe.

8. (B) Inference

Step 2: Identify the Question Type

The question asks for something researchers are "most likely to" accept, making this an Inference question.

Step 3: Research the Relevant Text

The question points directly to lines 30–31, but be sure to use the entire sentence and any surrounding sentences for context.

Step 4: Make a Prediction

In lines 30–34, the researchers in question are afraid that patent holders will demand high fees to use their materials for basic research. So, as a general rule, they would prefer it if patent holders were *not* allowed to charge such exorbitant fees.

Step 5: Evaluate the Answer Choices

(B) accurately addresses these researchers' concern.

(A) is a 180. Competition is what makes industries charge high fees for patented materials. These researchers oppose such a system.

(C) is a 180. These researchers *want* access to materials and are disgruntled about paying too much for them.

(D) is a Faulty Use of Detail. Fear of litigation is the first concern in paragraph 2. The researchers in lines 30–31 have a *different* concern: having to provide a lot of money in exchange for access.

(E) is a Faulty Use of Detail. Funding is mentioned in paragraph 1 as a reason why biotechnology researchers in academics support patents. The researchers in question though—from lines 30–31—are worried about what they have access to, not how much funding they receive.

9. (B) Detail

Step 2: Identify the Question Type

The phrase "[a]ccording to the passage" indicates a Detail question. The correct answer will be directly stated in the passage.

Step 3: Research the Relevant Text

The reason why university researchers support patents is described in paragraph 1.

Step 4: Make a Prediction

In lines 4–7, university researchers support patents "because of their reliance on research funding that is in part conditional on the patentability of their results."

KAPLAN

Step 5: Evaluate the Answer Choices

(B) is a perfect match.

(A) is Out of Scope. The passage never mentions the quantity or quality of their research.

(C) may be consistent with the author's point of view, but the passage never states that university researchers share this opinion.

(D) is Out of Scope. The passage never mentions partnerships between universities and corporations. It also never mentions any groups feeling "unfairly exploited."

(E) is Extreme. While some researchers (and maybe an increasing number—lines 4–5) may believe this, the passage never states that *most* researchers hold this view.

10. (C) Inference

Step 2: Identify the Question Type

This is an Inference question because it asks for something with which the author is "most likely to agree."

Step 3: Research the Relevant Text

The question asks about the author's point of view. That is found exclusively in paragraph 3, which makes it the most likely source of the correct answer.

Step 4: Make a Prediction

The author makes many points over the 25 lines of paragraph 3. Start with the overarching point (patents are not as problematic as some believe), eliminate answers that stray too far, and use content clues in the answers to perform any necessary research.

Step 5: Evaluate the Answer Choices

(C) is correct. In lines 47–51, the author states that litigation is expensive and would only be done to protect market position. Basic, noncommercial research wouldn't be worth the expense.

(A) is not supported. Lines 35–37 do suggest that materials were more freely shared in the early days, but it's never suggested that researchers weren't *entitled* to protection.

(B) is a Distortion. Some researchers fear such excessive fees (lines 30–34), but there's no indication that patent holders *typically* charge such fees.

(D) is another Distortion. Lines 6–7 confirm that academic institutions rely on such funding, but the author never expresses whether they rely "too heavily" on it.

(E) is Out of Scope. The concerns against patenting have to do with patent holders withholding access to useful materials. The innovative quality has no bearing on the issue.

11. (B) Logic Function

Step 2: Identify the Question Type

The phrase "primarily in order to" indicates a Logic Function question. Focus on *why* the author mentions the early days in context of the passage.

Step 3: Research the Relevant Text

The early days are mentioned in line 38, but the purpose of mentioning them is only seen by looking at the entire first sentence of paragraph 3. Also, consider how that sentence is used as a transition from paragraph 2.

Step 4: Make a Prediction

Paragraph 2 describes the concerns researchers have about patents. In the first sentence of paragraph 3, the author concedes that researchers have shifted to a market model. Nonetheless, researchers have always tried to protect their materials, "even in the early days." That phrase suggests that this is nothing new. You could go back to a time when ideas were exchanged more freely, but you'd *still* find some people trying to protect themselves.

Step 5: Evaluate the Answer Choices

(B) accurately describes how the phrase indicates that nothing is new. These kinds of practices have happened before.

(A) is a Distortion. Lines 35–37 do provide the absolute briefest account of any sort of evolution, but the *also* in line 37 suggests that the author included the reference to the early days to bring up a new point—not just to provide the history.

(C) is Out of Scope. The author expresses no such longing to return to the early days.

(D) is also Out of Scope. It brings up the level of technological sophistication, which is never mentioned here.

(E) is a 180. The author's point in paragraph 3 is that patents are fine, and the fact that some researchers have always wanted protection *supports* the idea that patents are acceptable.

12. (D) Inference

Step 2: Identify the Question Type

This is an Inference question because the passage provides "support for inferring" the correct answer.

Step 3: Research the Relevant Text

There are no content clues here, so the entire passage is relevant.

(C) is unsupported. The passage never suggests any action that universities would take on their own researchers.

(E) is part Extreme and part Out of Scope. The corporation *may* ask for something in exchange (lines 27–30), but there's nothing in the passage to suggest it *probably* will. Also, the passage does not suggest that a corporation would actively offer both funding and access to patented materials.

Step 4: Make a Prediction

Don't bother trying to predict the correct answer here. Eliminate answers that are clearly wrong, and use content clues in the answers to do any necessary research.

Step 5: Evaluate the Answer Choices

(D) is consistent with the second concern raised in paragraph 2. In lines 23–27, patent holders that do not sue can still "refuse to make such materials available" unless they get something in exchange.

(A) is an unsupported comparison. Policy makers (mentioned in line 13) may be scrutinizing patents more carefully, but there's no suggestion of how much they favor new restrictions or how that compares to what academic researchers believe.

(B) is Extreme. Lines 47–51 suggest that patent holders would sue only if they felt their market position threatened, but there's no indication that *most* patent holders actually feel threatened.

(C) is Extreme. Lines 4–7 suggest that funding is *partially* conditional on patentability, but that doesn't mean that academic institutions would be *unable* to get funding without patents.

(E) is Out of Scope. There is no mention of how many biologists are "willing to teach."

13. (D) Inference

Step 2: Identify the Question Type

This is an Inference question because it asks for something with which the author is "most likely to agree."

Step 3: Research the Relevant Text

The question asks about the author's point of view, which is all in paragraph 3. The question also refers to a situation involving "noncommercial research," a topic mentioned in lines 47 and 53.

Step 4: Make a Prediction

In lines 44–47, the author implies it's *questionable* whether patent infringement would be an issue in noncommercial research. First, the cost may not justify legal action in noncommercial situations; further, lines 51–54 suggest that courts have a tendency to grant exceptions to noncommercial research anyway. Therefore, the author most likely believes that the research described should not pose any problem.

Step 5: Evaluate the Answer Choices

(D) is correct. Even if a patent holder *does* try to sue, judges traditionally side with noncommercial research projects.

(A) is Extreme. Patent holders *may* demand high payment (lines 23–34), but that doesn't mean it will *probably* happen.

(B) is a 180. Lines 51–54 suggest that judges allow for exceptions in noncommercial cases.

Passage 3: Haudenosaune Wampum

Step 1: Read the Passage Strategically

Sample Roadmap

line #	Keyword/phrase	¶ Margin notes
4	primarily	Historians:
6	insisted … primarily	wampum = $
7	While	Auth:
9	due to	misinterpretation
10	misinterpreted	Wampum actually
12	However … true significance	political message
18	two	Loose beads
22	for example	= simple ideas
28	for example	Ex. communicate
35	thought that	with spirits
36	such that	String wampum = political message
37	however	Haud. Conf. made wampum
40	major impetus	primarily political
42	primarily	Wampum belts
43	evident	= depict rules
48	Ex	Belts indicate gov't business
58	Thus	
60	although	
61	effectively	

Discussion

Paragraph 1 starts right off with the **Topic**: wampum—beads used for mostly political communication by the Haudenosaune. Historians insist that wampum was primarily a form of currency, but the author asserts that this was a misinterpretation. This indicates that the **Scope** of the passage will be what wampum represents. The author's response to historians signals the **Purpose**: to clarify what wampum actually represents. And the phrase "true significance of wampum" gives away the **Main Idea**: Wampum was *not* supposed to be currency but instead a way of conveying messages, including important political ones.

Paragraph 2 begins to describe the chronological development of wampum's usage. Wampum was first used as loose beads, some white and some purple, to convey simple ideas. An example is given of how the beads represented different spirits and were used to communicate with these spirits. The Keyword [*l*]*ater* in line 33 indicates the next phase of wampum: string wampum. By stringing beads together, the Haudenosaune could send basic political messages.

Paragraph 3 introduces the next major stage, starting with the formation of the Haudenosaune Confederacy. The confederacy drafted a constitution, and its rules were encoded in wampum belts, which consisted of multiple wampum strings. Through a series of examples, it's shown how the wampum beads are arranged to indicate sociopolitical circumstances. Ultimately, wampum belts were successfully used as a way to "frame and enforce" confederate laws.

14. (B) Global

Step 2: Identify the Question Type

This is a Global question because it asks for the "main point" of each passage.

Step 3: Research the Relevant Text

No need to research any particular text here. The Main Idea from Step 1 will serve as a sufficient prediction.

Step 4: Make a Prediction

The point of the passage is that, despite what historians claim, wampum was *not* used primarily as currency but instead developed over time as a way to convey important information.

Step 5: Evaluate the Answer Choices

(B) is correct, saying that wampum was not intended as money and discussing the evolution of wampum as a form of communication. All of the details are accurate.

(A) is too narrow and a Distortion. Wampum started as just loose beads. Strings came [*l*]*ater* (line 33).

(C) is Extreme. While Europeans may have used wampum "solely to purchase goods" (line 11), that doesn't mean the Haudenosaune stopped using it as a form of communication. Thus, it was not *exclusively* used as a form of currency.

(D) is a Distortion. The establishment of the confederacy marked the beginning of wampum *belts*. But wampum was used before then in the form of loose beads and wampum strings.

(E) is another Distortion. It's fair to say that historians let the commercial use of wampum overshadow its communicative use in European transactions, but that doesn't mean they overlooked the communicative roles from *before* the Europeans arrived.

15. (E) Logic Function

Step 2: Identify the Question Type

The phrase "offered primarily as" indicates a Logic Function question. It's asking *why* the author mentions the fishing practice. As additional help, the question states that the fishing practice serves as an "instance of," i.e., an example.

Step 3: Research the Relevant Text

The fishing practice is described in lines 28–33. The phrase "for example" indicates that the practice illustrates the point made directly beforehand, so use the previous sentences for more context.

Step 4: Make a Prediction

Right before the claim about the fishing practice, the passage describes how the different colors represent different spirits. The phrase "for example" in lines 21–22 indicates that this is an example of the previous point: "Even in the form of loose beads, wampum could represent basic ideas." So ultimately, the fishing practice—which involves tossing loose beads into the water—is an example of how wampum in loose bead form could be used in such a way.

Step 5: Evaluate the Answer Choices

(E) is correct. Loose beads were the first stage in the evolution of wampum, and the fishing practice shows how loose beads were used.

(A) is a Faulty Use of Detail. The beads in this case were merely thrown into the water. Nothing was encoded until the development of wampum belts, as described in lines 43–45.

(B) is a Distortion. The Europeans may have changed historians' perception of how wampum was used, but there's no suggestion that the fishing practice itself was ever altered.

(C) is a Faulty Use of Detail. The Haudenosaune Confederacy didn't come about until 1451, *after* wampum was used only in loose bead form.

(D) is not supported. By line 28, the practice was described through *legend*. There's no indication that wampum was being studied when this legend was discovered.

16. (C) Logic Function

Step 2: Identify the Question Type

The phrase "serves primarily to" indicates a Logic Function question.

Step 3: Research the Relevant Text

The question asks about the last paragraph, so consider the entire paragraph. Margin notes will be useful.

Step 4: Make a Prediction

The last paragraph is all about how wampum evolved into belts, which represented the provisions of the Haudenosaune Confederacy.

Step 5: Evaluate the Answer Choices

(C) is correct. By creating belts, the wampum was used to symbolize constitutional provisions.

(A) is too narrow. While the paragraph does describe how wampum belts evolved from wampum strings (lines 45–48), that's just one sentence. This ignores the rest of the paragraph, which discusses the symbolic nature of the belts.

(B) is also too narrow. The comparison between belts and strings is found in lines 45–48, but this overlooks the rest of the paragraph, which discusses what the belts represent.

(D) is a Distortion. The author does provide several examples of wampum codes (lines 48–57), but they're just random samples. It's hardly a complete *outline* of the constitution.

(E) is a Distortion. The last sentence confirms that wampum was used *effectively*, but the paragraph only describes what wampum was *meant* to symbolize. It never actually gives *evidence* of its effectiveness. So, the paragraph's primary purpose was to tell *how* the wampum was used, not whether it ensured "compliance with the law."

17. (C) Inference

Step 2: Identify the Question Type

This question asks for what can be *inferred* and what the author is "most likely to agree with." That indicates an Inference question.

Step 3: Research the Relevant Text

There are no content clues, so the entire text is relevant.

Step 4: Make a Prediction

The correct answer here cannot be predicted. Instead, check the answers one at a time using content clues to do any necessary research.

Step 5: Evaluate the Answer Choices

(C) is supported. The association between colors and spirits is described before the Keyword [*later* (line 33), so it's definitely a precursor. And the later uses include "truce requests" (line 36) and "political purposes" (line 42), which do not utilize the spiritual associations.

(A) is not supported. Lines 7–11 indicate that wampum only became currency because of how Europeans misinterpreted it. There's no indication that Haudenosaune would have gone that route otherwise.

(B) is a 180. The use of colors was in the "simplest and oldest form of wampum" (lines 19–20), long before the confederacy.

(D) is a Distortion. While the associations may have changed once beads were formed into strings, there's no indication that color associations further changed when belts were introduced.

(E) is an unsupported hypothetical. Even if the Europeans *were* aware of the communicative role of wampum, they still could have just ignored that and used the wampum however they wanted.

18. (B) Inference

Step 2: Identify the Question Type

This is an Inference question because it asks for something the passage "provides the most support for inferring."

Step 3: Research the Relevant Text

There is no content clue here, so the entire passage is relevant.

Step 4: Make a Prediction

The correct answer cannot be predicted, so eliminate answers that are outside the scope of the passage, and use content clues to do any necessary research.

Step 5: Evaluate the Answer Choices

(B) is correct. The formation of the confederacy led to the invention of belts (lines 43–45), which were definitely more complex than the mere strings that were used before then.

(A) is a 180. Lines 7–11 suggest that wampum only developed an economic purpose because of European misinterpretation.

(C) is Out of Scope. There's no indication that the Haudenosaune ever stopped using wampum to represent the constitution or went on to use something else.

(D) is a subtle Distortion. While wampum *belts* were used to indicate and enforce edicts and policies, wampum could still have been used more often in other forms. It's possible that wampum strings were more common and used for purposes unrelated to the confederate policies. Line 4 does indicate that wampum was used primarily for political purposes, but to say wampum "served primarily" for official edicts and policies of the confederacy is not supported in the passage.

(E) is Out of Scope. In fact, lines 56–57 suggest that, even in belts, wampum still used the same "two colors" as always. Interpretation came from the *arrangements* of the colors, not different shades.

19. (E) Inference

Step 2: Identify the Question Type

This is an Inference question because it asks for something *inferred* that the author is "most likely to agree with."

Step 3: Research the Relevant Text

There are no content clues, so the entire passage is relevant.

Step 4: Make a Prediction

The correct answer cannot be predicted. Eliminate any answers that are clearly not supported, and use content clues to do any relevant research.

Step 5: Evaluate the Answer Choices

(E) is supported multiple times throughout paragraph 3. In the examples, the author says that longhouses *usually* meant a particular nation (line 49), fires *possibly* indicated talks (line 50), and lines "seem to have indicated" relationships (line 53). Those phrases all indicate inconclusive results.

(A) is Out of Scope. The passage never discusses objects similar to wampum, nor does it discuss what groups other than the Haudenosaune used.

(B) is a 180. The author states that Europeans "misinterpreted the significance of wampum," which suggests that they were not as aware as this answer suggests.

(C) is a 180. Line 11 states that Europeans used wampum "solely to purchase goods."

(D) is a 180 on multiple fronts. First, the use of wampum in loose bead and string form predated the Haudenosaune Confederacy. Only wampum *belts* seemed to come later. Also, the confederacy formed from "warring tribes" (lines 37–38), suggesting that any peaceful association was hardly *long term* when the belts were introduced.

Passage 4: Negative Evidence in Science

Step 1: Read the Passage Strategically

Sample Roadmap

line #	Keyword/phrase	¶ Margin notes
Passage A		
1	main	
2	power	negative evid. = disprove
3	fundamental point ... :	
4	for example	
5	but	
8	no value	can't prove
9	tantamount	
10	disproof ... Moreover	can disprove
11	At the heart	
13	not only ... but also	
15	Indeed ... only if	negative evid. vital
17	However	Auth rebuts
18	does not adequately	
20	But	Which premise disproved?
28	but	Negative evid.
31	never ... But	not conclusive
Passage B		
34		Predict Uranus orbit
41	incorrect	Failed
42	One possible explanation	
43	Incorrect ... Another	
44	error	Changed aux. assms.
45	changed	
46	concluding	
49		Found Neptune; prediction correct
53	Once again	Didn't predict Merc. orbit
54	hypothesized	
56	However ... never	No Vulcan—
58	Error ... Finally	Newton wrong?
62	rejection	
63	increased confidence	Einstein theory confirms

Discussion

Passage A starts off with Karl Popper's view of scientific evidence: positive evidence (i.e., supporting evidence) can never provide proof, but negative evidence (i.e., contradicting evidence) absolutely provides disproof. Based on that, Popper argues that negative evidence (**Topic**) is vital and that theories can't be truly scientific unless they're tested against negative evidence. The conclusive value of negative evidence is the **Scope** of the passage.

In paragraph 2, the author claims that Popper is ignoring reality. So, the **Purpose** is to refute Popper's claims. According to the author, scientific theories usually have multiple *auxiliary* assumptions. A failed prediction can just mean one of the assumptions was off—but which one is unknown. So, negative evidence isn't as conclusive as Popper suggests—which is the author's **Main Idea**.

Passage B discusses two experiments by astronomers. In the first, they tried to predict the orbit of Uranus using Newton's theories and auxiliary assumptions. The prediction failed, but they had assumed that there were no planets nearby. They changed the assumption, found Neptune, and the calculations worked. In the second experiment, they tried to predict Mercury's orbit. They failed again, and again changed the assumption—but no new planet was found. So, Einstein came up with a new theory, and all the calculations worked. Newton's theory was then rejected.

The **Topic** of passage B is predicting planetary orbits. The **Scope** is testing theories based on the results of predictions. The **Purpose** is merely describing what happened. The **Main Idea** is that, while Newton's theories held up in one situation, failed predictions and assumptions in another situation led to the rejection of Newton's theories.

While passage B never uses the term "negative evidence," the failed predictions in both experiments are perfect examples. So, both passages are ultimately focused on how negative evidence can be used to test theories. However, passage A is focused on scientific theories in general, while passage B stays focused on a specific scientific field—astronomy.

20. (C) Global

Step 2: Identify the Question Type

The question asks for the "central topic" of both passages, making this a Global question.

Step 3: Research the Relevant Text

For Global questions, there's no need to go back into the passages. The information gleaned from Step 1 will be enough to predict the answer.

Step 4: Make a Prediction

Both passages focus on testing theories and whether contrary (i.e., negative) evidence is enough to disprove them.

Step 5: Evaluate the Answer Choices

(C) is correct. Even though the phrase "negative evidence" never appears in passage B, the unexpected results described directly illustrate the concept.

(A) is mentioned in passage A, but passage B never discusses the relationship between positive and negative evidence.

(B) mentions planetary orbits, which are only focused on in passage B. Passage A never specifically discusses planets.

(D) brings up techniques for confirming a theory. Passage A only concentrates on using negative evidence, a technique for *disproving* theories.

(E) is a 180. Both passages suggest that experimentation is relevant, not irrelevant.

21. (C) Detail

Step 2: Identify the Question Type

The question asks for something *mentioned* in one passage and *illustrated* in the other. The correct answer will be directly stated somewhere, making this a Detail question.

Step 3: Research the Relevant Text

There are no content clues here, so the entire text is relevant.

Step 4: Make a Prediction

The experiments in passage B illustrate a few concepts from passage A. The failed prediction results are a prime example of "negative evidence" (seen throughout passage A). The assumptions about the existence of Neptune and Vulcan illustrate "auxiliary premises" (line 23 of passage A). The Uranus experiment illustrates that negative evidence isn't always conclusive (lines 30–32). And the rejection of Newton's theory illustrates that negative evidence *can* "disprove [theories]" (line 14). Any of these can be the correct answer.

Step 5: Evaluate the Answer Choices

(C) is correct, because passage A does mention disproving a theory (line 14), and passage B has the example of Newton's theory of gravity being rejected.

(A) is a Distortion. The theories that rely on experimental results can be repudiated, but there's no mention of disputing the results themselves.

(B) is illustrated by the Uranus experiment. However, revision is never mentioned in passage A.

(D) is illustrated twice in passage B, but passage A never mentions planets or their orbits.

(E) is referred to in passage A (lines 14–15 suggest that such theories are not truly scientific). However, the theories in passage B are all testable, so there's no illustration of one that's *not* testable.

22. (C) Inference

Step 2: Identify the Question Type

This is an Inference question because it asks for something that "most clearly illustrates" a term.

Step 3: Research the Relevant Text

Start by reviewing lines 22–26 for full context of what constitutes a "disturbing force." Then, use that to research passage B appropriately.

Step 4: Make a Prediction

Lines 25–26 discuss the "absence of" a disturbing force, and this is an example of an *auxiliary* premise. In lines 37–39, the author discusses an *auxiliary* assumption about the absence of planets near Uranus. So, the disturbing force would be "planets near Uranus," which is what Neptune is (lines 48–51).

Step 5: Evaluate the Answer Choices

(C) is a match.

(A) is a Distortion. Scientists made assumptions about the absence of planets *near* Uranus, not Uranus itself.

(B) is a Faulty Use of Detail. Astronomers had an assumption about the "mass of the sun" (line 36), not the absence of the sun.

(D) is a Distortion. In the second experiment, the scientists likely assumed the absence of planets *near* Mercury, not Mercury itself. Vulcan would be the kind of planet they originally assumed was absent.

(E) is Out of Scope. Passage B never mentions the moon.

23. (D) Inference

Step 2: Identify the Question Type

This is an Inference question because it asks for something the author "means to suggest."

Step 3: Research the Relevant Text

The phrase in question appears in line 7, but be sure to use the entire sentence for context. Then, the question asks about the author's opinion, which is found only in paragraph 2. Contrast Keywords [*h*]*owever* (line 17) and [*b*]*ut* (line 31) offer good places to check.

Step 4: Make a Prediction

In lines 6–10, Popper's "hyperbolic application" asserts that "negative evidence is tantamount to disproof." The word *hyperbolic* itself suggests an extreme point of view. Sure

enough, in lines 17–19, the author claims that Popper's application "does not adequately capture" what scientists actually face. And by lines 31–32, the author asserts that negative evidence is *not* conclusive, as Popper suggests. So, the author feels that the *hyperbolic* view is not as absolute as Popper suggests.

Step 5: Evaluate the Answer Choices

(D) matches the author's belief that Popper's view is "too radical" (*hyperbolic*) and not as conclusive as Popper thinks.

(A) is a Distortion. Popper applies the idea to scientific research, to which logical asymmetry *does* apply. The author just feels it's not always conclusive.

(B) is a 180. [*H*]*yperbolic* suggests *overestimation*. Popper thinks negative evidence will *always* disprove theories, but the author suggests that that's not always true.

(C) is a Distortion. The reasoning behind logical asymmetry is not in itself flawed. It's Popper's *application* of that reasoning that's extreme.

(E) is a Distortion. The idea of logical asymmetry *is* relevant, it just doesn't allow for the extreme conclusion that Popper suggests (i.e., positive evidence has no value, and negative evidence will always disprove).

24. (B) Inference

Step 2: Identify the Question Type

The question asks for what one author is "most likely to" do with information from the other passage. That makes this an Inference question.

Step 3: Research the Relevant Text

The correct answer will take something from passage B and support the last sentence of passage A. So, start with the last sentence of passage A (lines 31–32), and use that to research passage B appropriately.

Step 4: Make a Prediction

The last sentence of passage A claims that "negative evidence rarely is [conclusive]." There are three instances of negative evidence in passage B. In lines 40–41, results did not match predictions of Uranus's orbit. In lines 53–54, results did not match predictions of Mercury's orbit. In line 56, Vulcan was not found. However, the last two pieces of evidence *were* ultimately used to conclusively reject Newton's theory. Only the first results about Uranus's orbit were shown to be inconclusive, with Newton's theory holding up under new assumptions.

Step 5: Evaluate the Answer Choices

(B) is correct.

(A) is a Distortion. The discovery of Uranus (mentioned in line 33) didn't disprove or contradict any theory, as negative evidence would do.

(C) is a 180. This failure ultimately led to Newton's theory being rejected, suggesting that it *was* conclusive.

(D) is a 180. This failure *was* conclusive, destroying an assumption that led to the rejection of Newton's theory.

(E) is a Distortion. A successful prediction would be positive evidence. The last sentence of passage A is about the inconclusiveness of *negative* evidence.

25. (A) Logic Reasoning (Parallel Reasoning)

Step 2: Identify the Question Type

This is a Parallel Reasoning question because it asks for something in one passage that is "most analogous" to something in the other.

Step 3: Research the Relevant Text

The black swan is mentioned in lines 3–5. The developments leading to the rejection of Newton's theory are described in lines 52–64.

Step 4: Make a Prediction

The black swan is a piece of negative evidence that disproves the theory that "all swans are white." A parallel circumstance would involve a piece of negative evidence that disproved Newton's theory of gravity. Two pieces of negative evidence caused Newton's downfall: first, the failed prediction of Mercury's orbit (lines 52–54); second, the failure to find Vulcan (line 56). So, Mercury and Vulcan are the two bodies that played a role in disproving Newton's theory.

Step 5: Evaluate the Answer Choices

(A) is a match.

(B) is a 180. Newton's theory was upheld after new assumptions led to revised and confirmed predictions for Uranus.

(C) is a 180. The discovery of Neptune confirmed a new assumption that helped *validate* Newton's theory.

(D) is Out of Scope. Venus is never mentioned in the passage.

(E) is a Faulty Use of Detail. While there may have been assumptions about the "mass of the sun" (line 36), the sun was never mentioned in the evidence against Newton's theory.

26. (B) Inference

Step 2: Identify the Question Type

The question asks for something *inferred* that an author is "likely to be skeptical of." That makes this an Inference question.

Step 3: Research the Relevant Text

Without any content clues, all of the text is relevant.

Step 4: Make a Prediction

If the author of passage B would be skeptical about a claim, then there would be evidence to contradict that claim. The entire results of the Uranus experiment show that negative evidence is not conclusive and couldn't be used to disprove Newton. That contradicts Popper's claim in lines 9–10 that negative evidence is tantamount to disproof. The results of the Mercury experiment were used to disprove Newton's theory, so that questions the claim in lines 31–32 that negative evidence is rarely conclusive. And the fact that confirmed calculations "increased confidence in Einstein's theory" suggests that positive evidence *can* have value, as opposed to Popper's claim in line 8.

Step 5: Evaluate the Answer Choices

(B) is a match. By showing that positive evidence "increased confidence" in a theory, passage B suggests positive evidence *does* play a role.

(A) is Out of Scope. Passage B's examples address Popper's views, but never address whether these views were Popper's "main contribution" to science or not.

(C) is a 180. Both experiments described in passage B involve auxiliary assumptions. That would suggest agreement with this claim, not skepticism.

(D) is Out of Scope. Passage B never addresses logical asymmetry.

(E) is not supported. In both experiments described, negative evidence was found. But the author of passage B never suggests whether these experiments were an "attempt to refute" theories. Even if they weren't, passage B could still agree that scientific research involves both attempts to support *and* to refute theories.

27. (E) Logic Reasoning (Parallel Reasoning)

Step 2: Identify the Question Type

The correct answer asks for a situation "analogous to" one described in passage B. That makes this a Parallel Reasoning question.

Step 3: Research the Relevant Text

The discovery of Neptune is described in lines 44–51.

Step 4: Make a Prediction

In the experiment described, scientists were testing a theory by predicting the orbit of Uranus. The prediction failed because they assumed that no other planet was nearby. They then discovered Neptune, which *was* nearby. Once they factored that in, the calculations finally matched the prediction. The correct answer will contain a similar situation in another field of science: a theory is tested, but predictions don't match; something new is discovered, and that allows the predictions to be confirmed.

Step 5: Evaluate the Answer Choices

(E) is logically the same. A theory is tested (law of conservation of energy), but predictions don't match (combined energy was less than expected); something new is discovered (an undetected particle), and that allowed the prediction to be confirmed.

(A) does not match. Here, Galileo's predictions are shown to be wrong. In the passage, the discovery of Neptune allowed for a revision that helped *confirm* the predictions.

(B) is Out of Scope. This uses evidence to "settle a debate," which is something that is never done in passage B.

(C) does not match. Here, Alvarez makes a prediction and finds evidence to support the prediction. However, there's no mention of his prediction *not* matching in the first place.

(D) does not match. Here, Brunhes simply uses evidence to reach a conclusion. There is no theory tested and no unmatched predictions that are overturned by the discovery of something new.

Section II: Logical Reasoning

Q#	Question Type	Correct	Difficulty
1	Flaw	B	★
2	Inference	B	★
3	Point at Issue	C	★
4	Flaw	C	★
5	Assumption (Necessary)	C	★
6	Principle (Identify/Strengthen)	D	★
7	Paradox	C	★★
8	Method of Argument	E	★
9	Weaken	B	★★
10	Assumption (Sufficient)	B	★
11	Paradox	A	★★
12	Weaken	B	★★
13	Inference	D	★★
14	Strengthen	E	★★
15	Inference	A	★★
16	Flaw	C	★★
17	Inference	D	★★★
18	Assumption (Necessary)	B	★★★
19	Flaw	C	★★★
20	Paradox	E	★★★★
21	Parallel Flaw	B	★★★★
22	Assumption (Sufficient)	A	★★★
23	Principle (Identify/Strengthen)	E	★★★★
24	Assumption (Necessary)	D	★★★
25	Strengthen	D	★★
26	Principle (Parallel)	E	★★★

KAPLAN

1. (B) Flaw

Step 1: Identify the Question Type

The phrase "vulnerable to criticism" indicates that there's a flaw in the argument. Look for why the conclusion does not logically follow from the given evidence.

Step 2: Untangle the Stimulus

According to the evidence, industrial by-products can increase hormonal activity in reptiles. Some alligators were recently spotted with abnormalities that could only be caused by an increase in hormonal activity. So, the author concludes that there must have been industrial by-products in the swamp.

Step 3: Make a Prediction

The abnormalities had to be caused by increased hormonal activity, but industrial by-products are just one way of making that happen. By placing the blame solely on the by-products, the author overlooks other factors that could lead to the necessary hormonal activity.

Step 4: Evaluate the Answer Choices

(B) exactly describes what the author is overlooking.

(A) is Out of Scope. The alligators in question had the abnormalities that *are* caused by increased hormonal activity. There's no need to explain other abnormalities.

(C) is a 180. The author concludes that the by-products were in the "swamp's ecosystem," which *would* include any food eaten by the alligator. So, this is something that *is* considered—not overlooked.

(D) is an Irrelevant Comparison. Whether or not other animals had the abnormalities, the argument is about what caused these abnormalities in the first place.

(E) is Out of Scope. There's no information here about the exact number of alligators, so there's no basis to question the sample as unrepresentative. Besides, the argument is not about alligators in general, but about these specific alligators and their abnormalities.

2. (B) Inference

Step 1: Identify the Question Type

When a question asks for something that fills in a blank, look at the Keyword before that blank. In this case, the Keyword is [s]o, which means it will contain a conclusion. And a conclusion is meant to be an Inference based on the supporting evidence. (This is not a Main Point question because the conclusion is not actually stated—it needs to be inferred.)

Step 2: Untangle the Stimulus

According to the government official, it's good that foreign citizens cannot be cabinet secretaries because that position would require foreign citizens to perform duties they shouldn't be performing. As it turns out, cabinet undersecretaries would have to perform the same duties when the actual secretary is not around.

Step 3: Make a Prediction

The major point here is that foreign citizens should not be performing the duties of a cabinet secretary. If undersecretaries can be expected to perform those duties on occasion, then logic would dictate that foreign citizens should not hold the position of undersecretary either.

Step 4: Evaluate the Answer Choices

(B) is exactly what follows from the official's statements.

(A) is Out of Scope. There is no information here to support any granting of citizenship.

(C) is Extreme. While the official may conclude that *foreign* citizens should not be appointed as secretaries, there's no reason to exclude local citizens who have never served as undersecretaries.

(D) is a 180. The official directly states that it "is wise" that foreign citizens *not* serve as secretaries.

(E) is unsupported. The statements merely claim that undersecretaries *are* expected to stand in on occasion. There is no evidence given for why they *shouldn't*.

3. (C) Point at Issue

Step 1: Identify the Question Type

There are two speakers, and the question asks for a claim they "disagree over." That makes this a Point at Issue question.

Step 2: Untangle the Stimulus

Seeing that people in student government are all outspoken, Doris recommends more students to join so that they can become more outspoken. Zack points out a classic flaw in Doris's argument: student government doesn't *make* people more outspoken; those students were outspoken *before* joining.

Step 3: Make a Prediction

Zack's last sentence directly addresses the point at issue. Zack says joining student government will "do nothing" to make people more outspoken, contrary to Doris's suggestion.

Step 4: Evaluate the Answer Choices

(C) is the point at issue. Use the Decision Tree to confirm: 1) Does Doris have an opinion about this answer? Yes, she feels it *does* help. 2) Does Zack have an opinion about this? Yes, he feels it will "do nothing." 3) Are those opinions different? Absolutely.

(A) is certainly something that Doris favors. However, Zack offers no opinion on this. It's not that he feels students *shouldn't* be more outspoken, but that student government is not going to help.

(B) is exactly what Doris is encouraging. However, while Zack points out that becoming involved in student government won't help with making people outspoken, Zack could still encourage people to join for other reasons.

(D) is a 180 because this is something Doris and Zack agree on. They both state that student government people are outspoken. What they disagree on is what *made* them outspoken. Doris feels it was student government, while Zack says they were outspoken *beforehand*.

(E) is a Distortion. Zack would clearly disagree, but this logic distorts Doris's statements. **(E)** suggests that student government is the *only* way for students to become more outspoken. While Doris believes joining student government is sufficient, that doesn't mean students couldn't become more outspoken in other ways.

4. (C) Flaw

Step 1: Identify the Question Type

The given argument is said to be "vulnerable to criticism," which means this is a Flaw question. Determine why the evidence does not logically back up the conclusion.

Step 2: Untangle the Stimulus

Critics of a study of chameleons are complaining about the small sample size. The biologist concedes that point, but concludes that critics have no need to be skeptical. As evidence, the biologist refers to the reputation and status of the study's author.

Step 3: Make a Prediction

No matter how much expertise is involved, the study is still based on a mere six chameleons. Citing the author's credentials does nothing to address this concern. In short, the biologist is appealing to authority without providing any actual evidence.

Step 4: Evaluate the Answer Choices

(C) exactly expresses the appeal to authority flaw.

(A) is a possible flaw in the study, but the biologist does not make this mistake. The biologist's mistake is defending the study merely based on who conducted it.

(B) is irrelevant. The biologist has no need to explain this. The argument is merely about whether or not the results of the study are valid.

(D) mentions the critics' expertise, which is not relevant. The question is whether or not the study is valid based on its *author's* expertise, not how much expertise the critics have.

(E) is an Irrelevant Comparison. It doesn't matter how high the standards are for the critics. The biologist is only concerned about how well regarded the study's author is, and that's not relevant to whether the study is valid.

5. (C) Assumption (Necessary)

Step 1: Identify the Question Type

The question directly asks for an assumption, and one that is *required* by the argument. That makes this a Necessary Assumption question.

Step 2: Untangle the Stimulus

Despite what some analysts claim, the political scientist concludes that the government does *not* support freedom of expression. This is because the government recently accepted a protest pushing ideas the government supports, and governments that support freedom of expression would accept expressing ideas they support *and* oppose.

Step 3: Make a Prediction

The political scientist is suggesting that the government is playing favorites, only accepting protests with messages it supports. However, only the one protest is mentioned. There's no evidence of what the government would say to protests with a message it *doesn't* support. The political scientist assumes that the government would reject those protests, thus making the government not truly supportive of freedom of expression.

Step 4: Evaluate the Answer Choices

(C) must be true. After all, using the Denial Test, if the government *would* accept a protest with a message it opposed, then it would do everything a supportive government would, contradicting the political scientist's claim.

(A) is Out of Scope. The political scientist's argument does not require that the government actually help organize the rally. That may help strengthen the argument that the government plays favorites, but it's not needed. In order to confirm that the government does not truly support freedom of expression, something *is* needed to point at the government actually limiting that freedom.

(B) is Out of Scope. The argument is merely based on the government's support of the message, not the content of the message itself.

(D) is a Distortion. Groups don't have to *fear* government retaliation. Even if groups *weren't* afraid, the government could still be unsupportive of people expressing opposing ideas. **(D)** would strengthen the argument, but it's not required.

(E) is also not necessary. If the government *was* only acting out of fear of backlash, that could support the argument that the government isn't truly supportive. However, even if they *weren't* acting out of fear, the government could still be unsupportive of people expressing opposing ideas.

6. (D) Principle (Identify/Strengthen)

Step 1: Identify the Question Type

The question directly asks for a principle that will "justify the reasoning" provided. That means this is an Identify the Principle question that mimics a Strengthen question. Break the argument into evidence and conclusion, and look for a broadly worded answer that conforms to the argument's logic.

Step 2: Untangle the Stimulus

Convicted criminals are now being asked to pay a $30 "victim surcharge," which helps provide support for victims of violent crimes. Unfortunately, this fee is charged to *all* criminals. That may be fine for criminals who commit violent crimes, but the lawyer argues that this is unfair to criminals who commit less serious crimes, such as petty theft.

Step 3: Make a Prediction

As a general rule, the lawyer is arguing that criminals should not have to pay to support people affected by the more violent crimes of other criminals. The correct answer will be consistent with that principle.

Step 4: Evaluate the Answer Choices

(D) is a match.

(A) is Out of Scope. This argument is not about how severe the penalty is, but whether or not it's fair to make certain criminals pay it in the first place.

(B) is an Irrelevant Comparison. The argument is not about "overall penalties." It's only about a particular surcharge and who should have to pay it.

(C) is Out of Scope. The lawyer's claim of fairness is based on the type of crime committed, not how much of the $30 surcharge actually goes to the victims. So whether "all proceeds" are used for services is immaterial.

(E) is a Distortion. The lawyer is merely arguing that thieves should *not* pay the "victim surcharge." There's no mention of what fines they *should* pay.

7. (C) Paradox

Step 1: Identify the Question Type

The correct answer will *explain* something that occurred, making this a Paradox question.

Step 2: Untangle the Stimulus

According to the economist, the country in question is focusing more on services and less on manufacturing. With that, the country has reduced international trade.

Step 3: Make a Prediction

As with any Paradox question, ask "why." In this case, why would a greater focus on services lead to less international trade? It's not important to predict an exact answer, but know that the correct one will answer that question.

Step 4: Evaluate the Answer Choices

(C) provides an explanation. If markets for services were primarily local, then a country focusing on services would have less need to deal with outside markets.

(A) is a 180. If international trade covered manufactured goods *and* services, then the country's switch from one to the other should have made no difference.

(B) is an Irrelevant Comparison. The skills required for employment in either sector have nothing to do with international trade.

(D) is a Distortion. If a country wanted to cut back on unemployment, this may explain why it would shift focus to a more service-based economy. However, it does nothing to explain why international trade is going down.

(E) is a 180. If services were less expensive in other countries, then it would make sense to *increase* trade with those other countries. That makes the *decrease* in international trade even more inexplicable.

8. (E) Method of Argument

Step 1: Identify the Question Type

The word *by* is the key to recognizing this as a Method of Argument question. Simply put, the question asks for *how* Ortiz criticizes Merton (i.e., *by* doing what?).

Step 2: Untangle the Stimulus

Merton refers to a study that shows a greater rate of heart disease among people who live on busy streets. Merton argues that car exhaust pollution is to blame. Ortiz isn't convinced, suggesting that the people on those streets might just have unhealthy lifestyles.

Step 3: Make a Prediction

Merton is convinced that pollution is the cause, but Ortiz raises the question of an alternate cause. That questioning of possible alternatives is the Method of Argument.

Step 4: Evaluate the Answer Choices

(E) is correct. Ortiz suggests that Merton cannot be *sure* of pollution as the cause without ruling out the possibility of "other lifestyle factors."

(A) is a Distortion. Ortiz questions the conclusion Merton derives from the study, not the study itself.

(B) is a Distortion. Ortiz raises the question of other *causes* of heart problems, not other *effects* of air pollution.

(C) is not supported. There's no suggestion that Merton misunderstands the findings. What Ortiz questions is the conclusion Merton derives *from* those findings.

(D) is a Distortion. Merton does not draw a "general conclusion." Merton comes up with a specific conclusion about air pollution, and Ortiz counters with the general alternative possibility of "lifestyle factors."

9. (B) Weaken

Step 1: Identify the Question Type

The question directly asks for something that weakens the argument.

Step 2: Untangle the Stimulus

About 10 years ago, fish started to die out in two lakes: Quapaw and Highwater. At that point, fishing was banned at Quapaw but not at Highwater. Since then, the fish have returned at Quapaw, but fish numbers are still dwindling at Highwater. The author concludes that the fish population recovered at Quapaw because of the fishing ban.

Step 3: Make a Prediction

This is a classic case of Correlation versus Causation. Yes, the fish population happened to recover at the one lake with a fishing ban. But was the fishing ban really the cause? The author assumes so. To weaken that assumption, the correct answer will offer an alternative explanation or show how the fishing ban had no direct effect on the fish population.

Step 4: Evaluate the Answer Choices

(B) weakens the argument. If people weren't really fishing at Quapaw *before* the ban, then the fishing ban wouldn't have changed much. So, there must be another reason why the fish population recovered.

(A) might help explain why Highwater Lake continues to have troubles, but it doesn't offer any explanation why things improved at Quapaw Lake. The fishing ban is still a plausible explanation.

(C) is an Irrelevant Comparison. The size of the lakes has no bearing on why the fish population improved in Quapaw but not in Highwater.

(D) has no effect on the argument. Even if other lakes have seen increased fish populations, there's still the question of why. Maybe those lakes had fishing bans, too.

(E) is another Irrelevant Comparison. The argument is not about the number of *varieties* of fish but the total population overall.

10. (B) Assumption (Sufficient)

Step 1: Identify the Question Type

The question asks for something that, *if* assumed, would make the argument sound. That makes this a Sufficient Assumption question.

Step 2: Untangle the Stimulus

Because the Asian elephant always has some feet on the ground, the author concludes that it doesn't actually run.

Step 3: Make a Prediction

This is a fundamental case of Mismatched Concepts. The author's conclusion about running ability is based solely on evidence about feet being on the ground. The author assumes that any animal that keeps its feet on the ground cannot run. Or, as a contrapositive, any animal that *can* run must get all of its feet off the ground.

Step 4: Evaluate the Answer Choices

(B) is a match. If an animal needs to have all of its feet off the ground to run, then an animal that *doesn't* get all its feet off the ground (e.g., the Asian elephant) cannot run, as the author concludes.

(A) is a Distortion. The Asian elephant *can* accelerate, so this logic does not guarantee the author's conclusion.

(C) is an Irrelevant Comparison. It doesn't matter how fast the elephant is compared to other animals. The argument is about whether or not it can technically *run*.

(D) is Out of Scope. Saying the elephant's behavior is *unusual* has no bearing on whether it can run or not.

(E) is Out of Scope. Even if elephants were not alone in keeping their feet on the ground while *walking*, this does nothing to connect to the conclusion about whether they can run.

11. (A) Paradox

Step 1: Identify the Question Type

The question asks for something that will "explain [a] surprising result," making this a Paradox question. Look for the central mystery, and consider why things happen as they do.

Step 2: Untangle the Stimulus

A hardware store has two brands of hammers: Maxlast and Styron. Normally, the store sells an equal number of each. However, when the Maxlast brand was put on sale and displayed in the front of the store, people actually bought more Styron hammers.

Step 3: Make a Prediction

How bizarre. If people normally buy both hammers equally, one would think that placing Maxlast hammers in a more prominent location at a cheaper price would increase *that* brand's sale. So, why did people walk past them and buy more hammers of the other brand, which were still selling at full price? The correct answer will provide a reason why people passed on what should have been a great deal.

Step 4: Evaluate the Answer Choices

(A) offers an explanation. When people first enter the store, they don't pay close attention to the displays. So, people looking for a hammer wouldn't notice the display of cheaper Maxlast hammers and would walk on by. They would then head to the hammer section, where only one hammer brand remains: Styron.

(B) does not help. Neither the quality nor the service was said to change, so this wouldn't explain why people suddenly shifted their preference toward the one hammer *not* discounted and *not* displayed in the front. It's also too far a stretch to infer that the temporary lower price made people associate Maxlast with inferior quality, so it's still unclear why Styron was the bigger seller.

(C) does not help. The mystery is not why some people *did* buy Maxlast. The mystery is why more people *didn't*.

(D) is a 180. If the Maxlast hammer sale was advertised, it's even *more* unusual that a greater number of people opted for the Styron hammers.

(E) does not help. Even if people didn't make a special trip just to buy the hammer on sale, this still doesn't explain why, when people *did* go shopping there, they suddenly shifted to buying more Styron hammers.

12. (B) Weaken

Step 1: Identify the Question Type

The question directly asks for something that will weaken the given argument.

Step 2: Untangle the Stimulus

Two groups of mice were taught to navigate a maze. One group was given gingko, the other was not. The mice given gingko did better at remembering the maze a day later. Still, the author is skeptical, concluding that gingko was not the *direct* cause. As evidence, the author states that gingko reduces stress, and reducing "very high stress" could improve memory.

Step 3: Make a Prediction

If reducing stress in general helped improve recall, the author would have a solid argument. Then, gingko *would* be an indirect factor, only helping the mice by reducing their stress. However, the author only notes that reducing "very high stress levels" could improve memory. Perhaps reducing normal stress levels has no effect. In that case, if the mice in question weren't overly stressed to begin with, then it *is*

possible that gingko was the direct cause—contrary to the author's argument.

Step 4: Evaluate the Answer Choices

(B) weakens the argument. If none of the mice had very high stress levels, then there's no evidence that reducing their normal stress levels would have had any effect. That makes it possible that the gingko itself *was* the direct cause.

(A) is a 180. Even if the mice were given higher doses than needed, the gingko still could have reduced high stress levels, making gingko an *indirect* factor, as the author suggests.

(C) is irrelevant. Even if *some* such harmful substances exist, gingko did *not* impair the memory. So, this has no effect on whether gingko directly or indirectly aided in memory improvement.

(D) is Out of Scope. It doesn't matter what substances in ginkgo helped. If it helped reduce high levels of stress, it would still have an indirect effect, as the author claims.

(E) is also Out of Scope. The argument is not about how long it takes to *learn* the maze. The question is about what helped the one group of mice better *remember* the maze.

13. (D) Inference

Step 1: Identify the Question Type

The correct answer "must be true" based on the statements given, making this an Inference question.

Step 2: Untangle the Stimulus

There's just one claim here. Some politicians who supported free trade among Canada, the United States, and Mexico do *not* publicly support free trade with other Latin American countries.

Step 3: Make a Prediction

There's not much to deduce here. What's more important is understanding what this claim does *not* mention. The claim is about a group of people who supported the original free trade agreement. There's no information at all about politicians who *didn't* support that agreement, so the correct answer should not mention them. Also, the group in question does not publicly favor free trade with other Latin American counties. However, there's no information about anyone who *does* publicly favor such an extension of free trade. The correct answer should also exclude those people. All that's known is that a group of politicians exists who supported the initial free trade agreement but do *not* publicly support one with other Latin American countries. That also leaves the door open that they could support trade with other Latin American countries, just not *publicly*.

Step 4: Evaluate the Answer Choices

(D) must be true. If some politicians who favored the original deal do *not* publicly favor extending the deal, then it's impossible that every politician who favored the original deal publicly favors the new deal.

(A) does not have to be true. The original statement is about politicians who *did* favor the Canada-U.S.-Mexico deal but did *not* publicly favor the new Latin American deal. There's no information about politicians who *didn't* favor the original deal or ones that *do* publicly favor the new deal.

(B) does not have to be true. There's no information about politicians who *do* publicly favor extending free trade, so it's impossible to deduce whether they supported the original agreement or not.

(C) is a Distortion. Nothing suggests that these politicians changed their positions. They may have always refused to support free trade with other Latin America countries, while still supporting free trade among the original three. Another possibility is that they openly supported the first agreement, but are just silent in their support of the second agreement (i.e., they're refusing to support it *publicly*).

(E) is a Distortion. These politicians may not *publicly support* extending free trade, but that doesn't mean they actively *oppose* it. They may just keep quiet and reply "no comment" when asked.

14. (E) Strengthen

Step 1: Identify the Question Type

The correct answer will *justify* the application provided, which means it will strengthen the logic.

Step 2: Untangle the Stimulus

According to the principle, if someone commits copyright infringement, anyone who *knowingly* helps that person is also guilty. The application pronounces the Grandview Department Store guilty of copyright infringement because someone used its photo-printing kiosk to print a copyrighted photograph.

Step 3: Make a Prediction

By the principle, the department store would be guilty if it "knowingly aided" the person copying the photo. However, there's no evidence of that here. The correct answer will indicate how the store *knowingly* provided such aid.

Step 4: Evaluate the Answer Choices

(E) is correct. By this logic, because the department store provided a service that could lead to copyright infringement (the picture-printing kiosk), it "knowingly aided" the customer, justifying its guilt per the principle.

(A) is an Irrelevant Comparison. Copyright infringement likely *does* apply equally to full-service and self-service facilities.

However, this still provides no evidence that the store "knowingly aided" anyone.

(B) is Out of Scope. There's no evidence that the store *witnessed* the infringement. Even if it did, there's still the question of whether it "knowingly aided" the infringer.

(C) is also Out of Scope. There's no evidence that the store *didn't* post such a note. And if it did, this would make the store seem *less* liable. And note or not, there's still nothing indicating the store "knowingly aided" the copyright violator.

(D) is Out of Scope, too. There's no evidence that the store does *not* monitor the kiosk. And even if it didn't, this does not necessarily imply "knowingly aiding" the customer.

15. (A) Inference

Step 1: Identify the Question Type

The correct answer will complete the argument and fill in the blank. The blank ends a sentence that will be [o]bviously concluded from the preceding lines, making this an Inference question.

Step 2: Untangle the Stimulus

According to the author, the purpose of journalism is to help people make informed decisions. However, sensationalistic gossip provides information that is, for the most part, irrelevant.

Step 3: Make a Prediction

The conclusion will be about sensationalistic gossip. Because it does not provide relevant information for people, it does not serve the purpose of journalism described in the first sentence. The correct answer will note this non-journalistic quality of sensationalistic gossip.

Step 4: Evaluate the Answer Choices

(A) is a match.

(B) is a Distortion. While the gossip portion itself does not achieve the purpose of journalism, that doesn't mean it stops *other* portions of that newspaper or television news program from achieving journalism's purpose.

(C) is an Irrelevant Comparison. The stimulus has no comparison between current news and past news of any kind.

(D) is not supported. While this gossip does not qualify as journalism, it may certainly be considered a form of entertainment.

(E) is Extreme. The gossip may not be considered journalism, but it may still provide *some* value—e.g., perhaps it increases sales or viewership so more people are likely to consume the portions of the paper or news program that *do* have journalistic merit.

16. (C) Flaw

Step 1: Identify the Question Type

The question directly asks for the flaw in the argument.

Step 2: Untangle the Stimulus

A survey showed that 40% of people want Conservative legislators, 20% want Moderate legislators, and 40% want Liberal legislators. The author then concludes that most people want legislature to match those percentages.

Step 3: Make a Prediction

This is a gross misapplication of statistics. There's no evidence that people want to see a mixed legislature. They would probably prefer to see a legislature that is 100% their choice (e.g., 100% Conservative). The author is mistakenly taking the survey results of the entire group and assigning those numbers to each person.

Step 4: Evaluate the Answer Choices

(C) expresses the flaw of taking the group results and applying them to the individual responders.

(A) is a Distortion. The evidence *and* conclusion are about what people would "like to see," not about what is *actually* the case or what "should be" the case.

(B) is a Distortion. The conclusion uses the same numbers as the evidence, but the numbers are applied differently. There is no restated claim.

(D) is Out of Scope. The beliefs of the researchers are irrelevant to the author's misuse of statistical results.

(E) gets the details backward. The evidence is precisely quantified figures, while the conclusion mentions what is *roughly* the case. Regardless of which was precise and which was an estimate, the flaw still lies in the misapplication of statistics from individuals to the group—not in the switch from specific to approximate numbers.

17. (D) Inference

Step 1: Identify the Question Type

The question states that the given information will *support* the correct answer. Because the answer is being supported, this is an Inference question.

Step 2: Untangle the Stimulus

The city leader discusses two proposals: a tourism plan and a new automobile manufacturing plant. They would each create an equal number of jobs, and the tourism plan would bring in $2 billion. The manufacturing plant plan would cost more money, but the leader states that it would still be a reasonable expense.

Step 3: Make a Prediction

If it would be reasonable to spend money getting a new auto manufacturing plant, then spending *less* money on a proposal that would be equally, if not more, beneficial (i.e., the tourism plan) would have to be considered reasonable, too.

Step 4: Evaluate the Answer Choices

(D) is supported. If the auto plant idea is reasonable, then so is the tourism plan that would cost less, create the same number of jobs, and bring in a lot of money.

(A) is not supported. The leader only mentions the two options, of which the tourism plan is cheaper. However, there may be other options not mentioned, and the *least* expensive one may not be worth considering.

(B) is a Distortion. The leader finds it reasonable to reach out to *automobile* manufacturers, but that doesn't mean manufacturing plants "in general" are a good idea.

(C) is not supported. The leader mentions the relative cost of both plans, but never suggests the city can only afford one.

(E) is a 180. The leader directly states that a new automobile manufacturing plant would "create as many jobs" as the tourism plan.

18. (B) Assumption (Necessary)

Step 1: Identify the Question Type

The question asks for an *assumption* that the argument *requires*, making this a Necessary Assumption question.

Step 2: Untangle the Stimulus

The author urges people to not trust an article about patients who can predict changes to their medical status. As evidence, the author cites a similar claim that was ultimately disproven about more babies being born during full moons.

Step 3: Make a Prediction

For these cases to be *analogous*, as the author claims, the logic would have to be the same. The baby claim was deemed faulty because people were shown to have selective memory: they just remembered the busy nights during a full moon, not the busy nights without a full moon. To be analogous, the predicting patient claim would have to be faulty for the same reason: people just happen to remember when the patients' predictions are accurate, and not when the patients guess wrong.

Step 4: Evaluate the Answer Choices

(B) must be true for the analogy to hold. This suggests that, like the baby incident, medical staff have selective memory. They're less likely to remember patients who make predictions that don't happen. Instead, they're just more likely to remember the accurate predictions, fueling the rumor that patients are prophets. Using the Denial Test, if the medical staff *are* just as likely to remember the patients' predictions regardless of whether the predictions are accurate, then the selective memory analogy no longer holds.

(A) is not necessary. While the baby claim was "empirically disproven," the author still doesn't trust the article in question because it is based on anecdotal evidence. Also, even if empirical evidence to disprove the article is forthcoming, it certainly doesn't need to be disproven *soon*.

(C) is Out of Scope. It doesn't matter if the patients were serious or not. The analogy hinges on what the medical staff remembers and whether those stories can be trusted.

(D) is a Distortion. The point of the baby claim analogy is to show that people *thought* babies were born more during full moons. However, the suggestion is more likely that baby births were *equally* likely to be high with or without a full moon. The argument does not need it to be true that babies were born *less* under a full moon.

(E) is Out of Scope. The author's problem with the article is the reliability of anecdotal evidence, not how "widely held" the belief is.

19. (C) Flaw

Step 1: Identify the Question Type

The question asks why the reasoning is *flawed*, making this easy to identify as a Flaw question.

Step 2: Untangle the Stimulus

According to the politician, union leaders are upset about countries working together to control manufacturing. The concern is that this leads businesses to move labor to where worker protection is weak and wages are lower. Union leaders understandably want to stop this from happening. However, the politician argues that multinational control should *not* be stopped because union leaders are trying to protect their own interests.

Step 3: Make a Prediction

The problem is that the politician has no actual evidence to reject the union leaders' claims. The politician merely points a finger at their motives without actually addressing their claims. It's possible that their points are still valid even if they are looking out for their own interests.

Step 4: Evaluate the Answer Choices

(C) correctly points out how the politician rejects an argument merely because the outcome would benefit the union leaders themselves.

(A) is Extreme. The politician is merely rejecting this one argument about multinational control, not *all* viewpoints that union leaders express. For example, they may express some viewpoints that are not related to their self-interest, and the

politician would not be able to dismiss those based on the same reasoning.

(B) is Out of Scope and possibly Extreme. There's no mention of "political motivations." The union leaders are motivated by maintaining high worker wages. Furthermore, even if the union leaders' desire to keep wages high is somehow considered a political motivation, **(B)** says the politician assumes *anyone* with political motivations is unreliable, but the politician's reasoning may be just limited to union leaders.

(D) is not supported. There is no suggestion that union leaders don't have other arguments to back their claim. If anything, the politician *overlooks* any such arguments and focuses solely on union leaders protecting their interests.

(E) is Extreme. The politician is arguing against a particular group of union leaders. There's no suggestion that this argument extends to leaders of *all* unions. However, even if the politician does accurately attribute the viewpoint to *all* union leaders, the politician's argument is still flawed in that it fails to address their argument.

20. (E) Paradox

Step 1: Identify the Question Type

The correct answer here will *explain* a circumstance, making this a Paradox question.

Step 2: Untangle the Stimulus

Job prospects for chemistry majors are better than ever. Yet, over the past 10 years, while the number of students entering college as chemistry majors has stayed the same, fewer students are actually graduating with chemistry degrees.

Step 3: Make a Prediction

Paraphrase the paradox as a question of why: why are fewer students getting chemistry degrees if the number of students entering the program hasn't changed? Something must have changed in the past 10 years that is preventing an increasing number of students from graduating with the chemistry degree they went in for—and it's not dampened job prospects.

Step 4: Evaluate the Answer Choices

(E) provides an explanation. The classes have changed and become less appealing. In that case, students initially interested in chemistry may decide to bail in favor of something more exciting.

(A) doesn't help. This has probably always been true and wouldn't explain why the number of chemistry grads has *decreased* over the years. Those without the necessary background may not have been trying to major in chemistry in the first place.

(B) suggests that chemistry is not alone in its decreasing number of graduates, but still offers no explanation of *why* that's occurring. If anything, it adds more mystery. Why are those *other* departments suffering, too?

(C) could explain why some students change majors throughout college. However, it does not explain why it has happened significantly more often for chemistry majors over the 10-year period.

(D) makes an Irrelevant Comparison. It doesn't matter how chemistry job prospects compare to other sciences. Those job prospects for chemistry jobs are still the best they've ever been, so it's hard to understand why *fewer* students are graduating with chemistry degrees.

21. (B) Parallel Flaw

Step 1: Identify the Question Type

The correct answer will contain reasoning *parallel* to the reasoning in the stimulus, and that reasoning is described as *flawed*. That makes this a Parallel Flaw question. The correct answer must contain a flaw that is exactly the same as the one in the stimulus.

Step 2: Untangle the Stimulus

The author argues that human-borne diseases are probably not to blame for animal extinctions that occurred 46,000–56,000 years ago. Over 55 species disappeared, and no one disease could kill off that many species.

Step 3: Make a Prediction

The evidence adequately suggests that the extinctions were not caused by any one specific human-borne disease. However, the extinctions could have been caused by *several* human-borne diseases, each responsible for some extinctions. The correct answer will commit the same logical error: suggesting a whole group of entities cannot accomplish something because no single member could accomplish it alone, ignoring the possibility of multiple members working together.

Step 4: Evaluate the Answer Choices

(B) makes the same mistake. This argument suggests that a group of entities (the two people involved) cannot accomplish something (repair the apartment) because no one member could fix both the door and window. It ignores the possibility that the apartment can be fixed by *both* of them, each responsible for one task. Although it does not match the level of certainty by omitting a word parallel to the word *probably*, it does contain the same group vs. member flaw.

(A) rejects something as the cause of a problem, but does not generalize about a group based on what one individual member cannot do.

(C) does reject the possibility of dinner by using the fact that no single restaurant appeals to everyone. However, it makes no sense that they would go to *multiple* restaurants for dinner together, so this doesn't match the overlooked possibility of the stimulus.

(D) is, among other problems, backward. The original argument used evidence about individual diseases to make a conclusion about a group of diseases. **(D)** uses evidence about a group of art to make a conclusion about an individual piece of art.

(E) is flawed because, even though the vaccine does help some people, it still *could* be correct that some people get no benefit from it. However, this is not the same logic as the stimulus. It draws no conclusion about a group of entities based on individual members.

22. (A) Assumption (Sufficient)

Step 1: Identify the Question Type

This question asks for something *assumed*, and the argument will be logical *if* that assumption is included. That makes this a Sufficient Assumption question.

Step 2: Untangle the Stimulus

A tax preparation company puts a particular disclaimer on all of its emails. However, the author argues that the disclaimer has no purpose. After all, if an email were to encourage something illegal, the disclaimer would not provide legal protection, which would be the sole purpose of such a disclaimer.

Step 3: Make a Prediction

The author has a point, *if* the email were to encourage something illegal. In that case, it wouldn't provide any legal protection, and would thus fail to serve its only purpose. But what if an email *doesn't* encourage anything illegal? In that case, the disclaimer may provide legal protection and thus could serve some purpose. The author suggests otherwise, assuming that the disclaimer wouldn't provide legal protection in *either* case, whether the email encouraged something illegal or not.

Step 4: Evaluate the Answer Choices

(A) completes the argument. As the author states, the disclaimer provides no protection when emails *do* encourage illegal activities. If, as this suggests, there's no protection needed when emails *don't* encourage illegal activities, then the disclaimer has no effect and thus serves no purpose, as the author claims.

(B) doesn't help. Even if the company is subject to penalties when emails encourage illegal activity, that still doesn't confirm that the disclaimer serves no purpose on other emails.

(C) is Out of Scope. The argument is about the disclaimer serving its purpose of offering legal protection, which is not based on whether the client ignores the message or not.

(D) is irrelevant. Sure, emails that encourage illegal activities are still not legally protected if people actually followed the advice. But this fails to address emails that do *not* encourage illegal activities. Disclaimers in those emails could still provide protection, whether people follow the advice or not.

(E) is Out of Scope. Customer behavior doesn't matter. This still ignores what would happen if emails did *not* encourage illegal behavior. The disclaimer in those emails could still provide some protection from those people who would perform illegal tax activities if they could.

23. (E) Principle (Identify/Strengthen)

Step 1: Identify the Question Type

The correct answer will be a principle, making this an Identify the Principle question. Because the principle will "support the reasoning" provided, it also acts as a Strengthen question. Validate the argument by finding an answer that conforms to the logic in broader terms.

Step 2: Untangle the Stimulus

Some people *try* to help their friends who are having marital problems, but they usually fail. Thus, the author concludes that these people's actions are unjustified.

Step 3: Make a Prediction

That's a rather harsh judgment. The author is basically saying that, even if people mean well, their actions are unjustified if they don't succeed. In other words, actions are justified *only if* they actually help.

Step 4: Evaluate the Answer Choices

(E) broadly summarizes the author's judgment that actions are not justified unless they actually help.

(A) is irrelevant. It doesn't matter *how* good the intentions are. The author still claims that such attempts are "usually ineffectual" and unjustified if unsuccessful.

(B) is a 180. The consequences are all that matter to the author.

(C) is a Distortion. All that matters to the author is whether the problem gets solved or not—regardless of intention.

(D) is a Distortion. Per the author, intentions are certainly irrelevant to deeming an action *unjustified*. However, the author doesn't mention what kinds of actions *are* justified. So, adding **(D)** wouldn't help determine whether the specific attempts to resolve the marital problems of one's friends are justified or unjustified.

24. (D) Assumption (Necessary)

Step 1: Identify the Question Type

The question asks for an *assumption* that is *required*, making this a Necessary Assumption question.

Step 2: Untangle the Stimulus

This argument opens with someone else's claim: authors who try to please their readers cannot produce books that impart truth. The argument's evidence attempts to explore the implications of that claim. If the claim were true, then a book's truthfulness could be judged by its sales figures, because a popular book must give pleasure, and thus must be at least partially untrue. On the basis of that reasoning, the argument concludes by rejecting the claim: authors who try to please their readers *can* produce books that impart truth.

Step 3: Make a Prediction

The argument's reasoning has several holes in it. Turn the argument's "What if?" strategy against it. What if readers purchase or read books without knowing whether the book will please them, or what if they sometimes choose to read books they know will not please them? Then sales figures and popularity wouldn't indicate readers' pleasure. What if books fail to please even when authors wrote them with the intention to please? Result and intention are not the same thing, yet the argument assumes that they are. Finally, what if a book could give pleasure even if the author had not tried to please the reader? If that were true, the argument's central premise falls apart. Here again, the argument treats an author's intentions and a book's results as equivalent.

Step 4: Evaluate the Answer Choices

(D) is one of the argument's central assumptions, saying that books that give readers pleasure *must* be written with that intention. If books can produce pleasure even if their authors did not try to please their readers, then the argument's rejection of the original claim would be invalid.

(A) is a 180. By equating sales figures with pleasure, the argument assumes that people do choose to read books that they know will give them pleasure.

(B) is a 180. The argument assumes that books that give pleasure *are* indicative of an author's intention to give pleasure.

(C) is Out of Scope. The argument is about whether or not the books *can* impart truth, regardless of readers' concerns.

(E) is a 180. The argument assumes that popularity and pleasure are equivalent.

25. (D) Strengthen

Step 1: Identify the Question Type

The question directly asks for something that will strengthen the given argument.

Step 2: Untangle the Stimulus

The author argues that most new shows by Wilke & Wilke will be canceled. As evidence, the author cites their poor record from the previous year. Also, their new shows are all police dramas, which have not done so well lately.

Step 3: Make a Prediction

The author is making a prediction based on past performance. Predictions always assume constancy. In other words, the author assumes that there's no drastic change or difference that would impact the prediction. So, to strengthen the prediction that Wilke & Wilke will fail, the correct answer will validate that Wilke & Wilke are offering nothing new that would suggest a different outcome.

Step 4: Evaluate the Answer Choices

(D) helps the author out. Not only are Wilke & Wilke trotting out a relatively unpopular genre, but they're repeating a strategy that provided no success at all for them last year. That suggests a continued struggle for Wilke & Wilke.

(A) is an Irrelevant Comparison. The author concluded that *most* of their new shows would be canceled. That's over half, regardless of the quantity produced. If Wilke & Wilke increased their production, perhaps they have a better chance this year of having *some* more shows stick around—but not a better chance of the majority doing so.

(B) doesn't help. Even if, last year, most of their shows were cancelled and most of their shows were police dramas, then it could only be inferred that *some* of their police dramas were canceled. However, their biggest success story from last year may have been a police drama. By putting all their efforts there, maybe they can repeat the magic and go against the author's claim.

(C) is Out of Scope. This indicates that last year Wilke & Wilke only succeeded with shows other than police dramas. They aren't making any shows like that this year, so this information is irrelevant to the new lineup of all police dramas.

(E) is Extreme. Even if the *most* popular shows weren't police dramas, some police dramas could have been popular enough to warrant trying out a few new ones.

26. (E) Principle (Parallel)

Step 1: Identify the Question Type

The question asks for something that *conforms* to a principle. However, the principle is not given but merely *illustrated* by

the stimulus. So, this is a Parallel Principle question. Start by identifying the general rule behind the argument in the stimulus, then find an answer that is logically consistent with that principle.

Step 2: Untangle the Stimulus

The author is concerned about a company that profited from committing fraudulent acts. The author argues that the company should be penalized to compensate for those profits.

Step 3: Make a Prediction

The author's general problem is seeing profit coming from misdeeds. The correct answer will provide another specific example of someone who shouldn't be allowed to profit from wrongdoing.

Step 4: Evaluate the Answer Choices

(E) is a match. Like the corporation, the convicted criminal is able to profit from a misdeed. And like the original argument, this recommends a course of action that will prevent the criminal from profiting.

(A) suggests a penalty that will prevent a recurrence of the original misdeed. However, the original argument was not concerned with recurrence, and this argument makes no mention of profiting.

(B) also places a penalty to safeguard against recurrence, which is not the same as the original. Also, there's no indication that the money is meant to "offset any profit."

(C) is not a match. The original argument is concerned about the penalty itself, not who benefits from the penalty.

(D) does not match. The penalty here is more about taking away a future privilege than offsetting a previous benefit.

Section III: Logic Games

Game 1: Recruiting Criminal Accomplices

Q#	Question Type	Correct	Difficulty
1	Acceptability	D	★
2	Partial Acceptability	C	★
3	"If" / Could Be True	D	★
4	"If" / Must Be False (CANNOT Be True)	B	★
5	"If" / Could Be True	A	★
6	"If" / Must Be True	B	★

Game 2: Newspaper Photographs

Q#	Question Type	Correct	Difficulty
7	Acceptability	B	★
8	"If" / Must Be True	C	★
9	"If" / Must Be True	D	★
10	Could Be True	A	★★
11	"If" / Could Be True	C	★★
12	"If" / Could Be True	E	★★★
13	"If" / Could Be True	C	★★

Game 3: Campus Art Gallery

Q#	Question Type	Correct	Difficulty
14	Partial Acceptability	A	★
15	Must Be True	C	★★★
16	"If" / Must Be True	B	★★★★
17	"If" / Could Be True	E	★★★★
18	"If" / Could Be True	B	★★★

Game 4: Publishing Cookbooks

Q#	Question Type	Correct	Difficulty
19	Acceptability	E	★
20	"If" / Could Be True	C	★
21	"If" / Could Be True	B	★
22	Completely Determine	A	★★
23	Rule Substitution	B	★★★

Game 1: Recruiting Criminal Accomplices

Step 1: Overview

Situation: A detective investigating when a criminal recruited a series of accomplices

Entities: Seven accomplices (Peters, Quinn, Rovero, Stanton, Tao, Villas, White)

Action: Strict Sequencing. Determine the order in which the accomplices were recruited.

Limitations: Each accomplice was recruited "one at a time," so this is a standard one-to-one Sequencing game.

Step 2: Sketch

The words "immediately before" in the first rule and an established position in the fourth rule indicate that this is Strict Sequencing. So, list the entities by initial, and set up seven numbered slots in order.

P Q R S T V W

‾1‾ ‾2‾ ‾3‾ ‾4‾ ‾5‾ ‾6‾ ‾7‾

Step 3: Rules

Rule 1 prevents Stanton and Tao from being recruited consecutively, in either order.

| S T | T S |

Rule 2 provides a relative sequence: Quinn is recruited some time before Rovero.

Q . . . R

That means Quinn cannot be the last accomplice recruited, and Rovero cannot be the first. Add "~ Q" and "~ R" under the respective slots.

Rule 3 creates a Block of Entities: Villas is recruited immediately before White.

| V W |

That means Villas cannot be the last accomplice recruited, and White cannot be the first. Add "~ V" and "~ W" under the respective slots.

Rule 4 establishes Peters as the fourth recruit. Add P to the fourth slot in the sketch.

Step 4: Deductions

Deductions are scarce in this game. There is one Block of Entities (Villas and White), but it can be placed in any pair of positions before or after Peters. There is no clear source of Limited Options. There is one Established Entity: Peters. That provides a couple of minor deductions. With Peters fourth, Villas cannot be third (because that would not allow White to be immediately after, as Rule 3 dictates), and White cannot be fifth (because that would not allow Villas to be immediately before, as Rule 3 dictates). There are no Numbers issues here, and there are no Duplications. Every

entity is mentioned in the rules, so there are no Floaters. Thankfully, the game consists of two Acceptability questions and four New-"If" questions—a good sign that few deductions were expected in the first place. Going into the questions, the Master Sketch should look something like this:

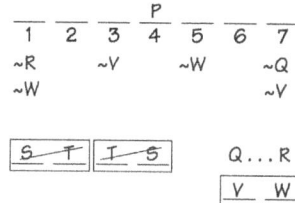

			P			
‾1‾	‾2‾	‾3‾	‾4‾	‾5‾	‾6‾	‾7‾
~R		~V		~W		~Q
~W						~V

| S T | T S | Q . . . R

| V W |

Step 5: Questions

1. (D) Acceptability

As with any Acceptability question, use the rules one at a time to eliminate answers that violate those rules.

(A) violates Rule 1 by having Stanton immediately after Tao.
(E) violates Rule 2 by having Quinn after, not before, Rovero.
(B) violates Rule 3 by having Villas and White separated (and in the wrong order). **(C)** violates Rule 4 by having Peters fifth instead of fourth. That leaves **(D)** as the correct answer.

2. (C) Partial Acceptability

As with standard Acceptability questions, the four wrong answers will be unacceptable because they will violate the rules. Start by using the rules one at a time to test the answers. If there are multiple answers remaining, start considering where the unlisted accomplices would be placed.

None of the answers directly violate Rules 1 or 2. **(B)** violates Rule 3 by not having Villas immediately before White. **(E)** violates Rule 4 because the answers list the accomplices recruited from second to sixth, which includes the fourth accomplice, but Peters is not listed.

From there, test the remaining answers by using the rules to determine where the unlisted entities would be placed. Remember that these answers list the accomplices from second to sixth, so the unlisted entities must be placed first and seventh.

(A) does not include Rovero or White. Rovero must be recruited after Quinn (Rule 2), and White must be recruited after Villas (Rule 3). That would leave nobody to be first, so this list is unacceptable.

(C) does not include Rovero or Tao. Rovero must be recruited after Quinn (Rule 2), so Rovero could be placed seventh. That would place Tao first, which is far enough away from Stanton.

T	V	W	P	Q	S	R
1	2	3	4	5	6	7

That would all be acceptable, making this the correct answer. For the record:

(D) does not include Quinn or Tao. Quinn must be recruited before Rovero (Rule 2), so Quinn would have to be first. That would place Tao seventh, but that would place Tao immediately after Stanton. That violates Rule 1, making this unacceptable.

3. (D) "If" / Could Be True

For this question, Tao is recruited second.

$$\frac{\ \ }{1}\ \frac{T}{2}\ \frac{\ \ }{3}\ \frac{P}{4}\ \frac{\ \ }{5}\ \frac{\ \ }{6}\ \frac{\ \ }{7}$$

By Rule 1, Stanton cannot be recruited first or third, so Stanton must be one of the last three accomplices recruited. There must be two consecutive spaces for Villas and White, so they must be recruited either fifth and sixth or sixth and seventh. Either way, they will take up the last three spaces along with Stanton. That leaves Quinn and Rovero, in that order (Rule 2), to be first and third. Because Villas and White are a block, Stanton cannot come in between them, so draw out the two possibilities:

I) $\frac{Q}{1}\ \frac{T}{2}\ \frac{R}{3}\ \frac{P}{4}\ \frac{S}{5}\ \frac{V}{6}\ \frac{W}{7}$

II) $\frac{Q}{1}\ \frac{T}{2}\ \frac{R}{3}\ \frac{P}{4}\ \frac{V}{5}\ \frac{W}{6}\ \frac{S}{7}$

With that, Villas could be sixth, making **(D)** the correct answer.

4. (B) "If" / Must Be False (CANNOT Be True)

For this question, Quinn and Rovero become a block. By Rule 2, Q would be before R (QR). Along with Villas and White (Rule 3), there are now two blocks that need to fit into the sketch. With Peters fourth, there are only three spaces before Peters and three spaces after. It is impossible to place both blocks before or after Peters. Therefore, one block must be placed before Peters and one block after. It doesn't matter which block goes where.

However, when one block is placed before Peters, it will go either first and second or second and third. Either way, the block must overlap the second position. Similarly, the block after Peters will go either fifth and sixth or sixth and seventh. Either way, that block must overlap the sixth position.

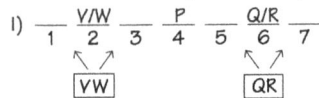

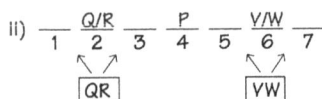

I) $\frac{\ \ }{1}\ \frac{V/W}{2}\ \frac{\ \ }{3}\ \frac{P}{4}\ \frac{\ \ }{5}\ \frac{Q/R}{6}\ \frac{\ \ }{7}$
       ↖ ↗   ↖ ↗
       [VW]   [QR]

II) $\frac{\ \ }{1}\ \frac{Q/R}{2}\ \frac{\ \ }{3}\ \frac{P}{4}\ \frac{\ \ }{5}\ \frac{V/W}{6}\ \frac{\ \ }{7}$
       ↖ ↗   ↖ ↗
       [QR]   [VW]

Stanton is not part of either block, so Stanton will never be in one of the positions taken up by either block. So, Stanton can never be second or sixth. That makes **(B)** the correct answer.

5. (A) "If" / Could Be True

For this question, White is recruited before Rovero, and Rovero is recruited before Tao. By Rule 3, Villas must be recruited immediately before White. Altogether, this creates a long string of entities:

[VW] . . . R . . . T

With Peters taking up the fourth spot, the block of Villas and White is restricted. It cannot be placed after Peters, because there would not be enough room after it for both Rovero and Tao. So, the block must be placed before Peters, either first and second or second and third:

I) $\frac{V}{1}\ \frac{W}{2}\ \frac{\ \ }{3}\ \frac{P}{4}\ \frac{\ \ }{5}\ \frac{\ \ }{6}\ \frac{\ \ }{7}$

II) $\frac{\ \ }{1}\ \frac{V}{2}\ \frac{W}{3}\ \frac{P}{4}\ \frac{\ \ }{5}\ \frac{\ \ }{6}\ \frac{\ \ }{7}$

By Rule 2, Quinn must also be recruited before Rovero, so that creates a string of Quinn, Rovero, and Tao, in that order (Q … R … T). That leaves Stanton, who cannot be placed next to Tao (Rule 1). Stanton cannot come last, or else he would be next to Tao. Stanton also cannot be sixth, because then Tao would be last and they would still be consecutive. So, the last two accomplices recruited must be Rovero and Tao, in that order. Then, Quinn and Stanton can take up the remaining positions, in either order.

I) $\frac{V}{1}\ \frac{W}{2}\ \frac{Q/S}{3}\ \frac{P}{4}\ \frac{S/Q}{5}\ \frac{R}{6}\ \frac{T}{7}$

II) $\frac{Q/S}{1}\ \frac{V}{2}\ \frac{W}{3}\ \frac{P}{4}\ \frac{S/Q}{5}\ \frac{R}{6}\ \frac{T}{7}$

With that, Quinn could be first, making **(A)** the correct answer.

6. (B) "If" / Must Be True

For this question, White is recruited immediately before Quinn. This creates a three-entity block with Villas, White, and Quinn (VWQ). With Peters fourth, there are only two places to add a three-entity block: first through third or fifth through seventh. However, the block includes Quinn, who must be recruited before Rovero (Rule 2).

[VWQ] . . . R

So, the block cannot be at the end, which means it must be first through third.

That leaves Rovero, Stanton, and Tao to be the last three accomplices recruited. Stanton and Tao cannot be recruited consecutively (Rule 1), so Rovero has to come in between them. That would place Stanton and Tao fifth and seventh, in either order, with Rovero in the middle at sixth.

I) $\frac{V}{1}\ \frac{W}{2}\ \frac{Q}{3}\ \frac{P}{4}\ \frac{S/T}{5}\ \frac{R}{6}\ \frac{T/S}{7}$

The sixth accomplice must be Rovero, making **(B)** the correct answer.

Game 2: Newspaper Photographs

Step 1: Overview

Situation: A newspaper choosing photos for its next edition

Entities: Three sections (Lifestyle, Metro, Sports) and three photographers (Fuentes, Gagnon, Hue)

Action: Matching. Determine which photographer's photos will be assigned to each section. (While some may label this game something other than Matching, understanding the general action would ultimately lead to the same sketch. Those skills should prevail over worrying about the exact categorization.)

Limitations: Each section will have exactly two photographs, which means there will be six photographs in total. With only three photographers to assign, at least one photographer will be assigned multiple times. However, the overview never states that each photographer *will* be assigned. That's not mentioned until the first rule. Be careful about making such assumptions. This game is forgiving, but other games *can* include entities that are never used. Also note that the overview never states that the two photographs in a section are taken by different photographers. Thus, for example, it is possible that the two photographs in the Lifestyle section are both taken by Fuentes.

Step 2: Sketch

The sections are more fixed, with the photographers being more variable. Plus, in context of the situation, it makes more sense to assign photographers to the different sections. So, list the photographers by initial, and set up a chart with a column for each section. Draw two slots in each column to assign the photographers.

$$\begin{array}{c} \text{F G H} \\ \begin{array}{c|c|c} \text{Lif} & \text{Met} & \text{Spo} \\ \hline \underline{} & \underline{} & \underline{} \\ \underline{} & \underline{} & \underline{} \end{array} \end{array}$$

Step 3: Rules

Rule 1 sets some limitations on the photographers. Each one will be assigned at least once, but cannot be assigned more than three times. Make a note of that to the side in shorthand:

Each pho. 1–3x

Rule 2 states that at least one photographer has to be assigned to both Lifestyle and Metro. Either set one slot in Lifestyle equal to a slot in Metro (adding "=" between them across the column), or set a note to the side:

At least 1 Lif = 1 Met

Rule 3 creates a numeric restriction: the number of photos by Hue in Lifestyle must be equal to the number of photos by Fuentes in Sports. Make a note of that to the side:

$$\# \frac{\text{Lif}}{\text{H}} = \# \frac{\text{Spo}}{\text{F}}$$

Rule 4 prevents Gagnon from being assigned to Sports. Draw "~ G" under the Sports column.

Step 4: Deductions

Each of the first three rules has a numeric component, which means Numbers will be important in this game. By Rule 1, each photographer will be used at least once, but no more than three times. With three photographers and six spots, there are only two ways to arrange the numbers: 1) Each photographer is assigned twice. 2) One photographer is assigned once, another twice, and the last one three times (2:2:2 or 1:2:3). While worth noting, this does not provide any concrete deductions.

By Rule 2, at least one photographer must be assigned to both the Life and the Metro section, but that could be any of the three. Rule 3 offers the best chance at some deductions.

By Rule 3, there must be an equal number of photos by Hue in the Lifestyle section as there are by Fuentes in the Sports section. There are only three possible outcomes for that number: 0, 1, or 2. Each outcome would establish substantial information, so it may be worth considering a rare foray into three Limited Options.

A quick glance ahead at the questions indicates that five out of the seven questions are New-"If" questions. So, while Limited Options can be helpful, the numerous "if" questions allow for enough sketching to make this game equally manageable without them. If you do set up Limited Options, here's what would happen:

$$\text{I)}\quad \begin{array}{c|c|c} \text{Lif} & \text{Met} & \text{Spo} \\ \hline \text{F/G} & \text{F/G} & \text{H} \\ \text{F/G} & \underline{} & \text{H} \end{array}$$

In the second option, there would be one photo by Hue in Lifestyle and one photo by Fuentes in Sports. Because there are no photos by Gagnon in Sports (Rule 4), the second photo in Sports would have to be by Hue. The second photo in Lifestyle could be by Fuentes or Gagnon. Any photographer could be the one assigned to both Lifestyle and Metro. No further deductions can be made.

$$\text{II)}\quad \begin{array}{c|c|c} \text{Lif} & \text{Met} & \text{Spo} \\ \hline \text{H} & \underline{} & \text{F} \\ \text{F/G} & \underline{} & \text{H} \end{array}$$

In the third option, there would be two photos by Hue in Lifestyle and two photos by Fuentes in Sports. Because Hue is the only photographer assigned to Lifestyle, Hue must have at least one photo in Metro (Rule 2). That leaves one photo in Metro, which has to be assigned to Gagnon, who is the only photographer not yet assigned.

III)	Lif	Met	Spo
	H	H	F
	H	G	F

Step 5: Questions

7. (B) Acceptability

As with any Acceptability question, go through the rules one at a time, eliminating answers that violate those rules.

(E) violates Rule 1 by including *four* photographs by Hue (one in Lifestyle, two in Metro, one in Sports). **(C)** violates Rule 2 by not having a photographer in common between Lifestyle and Metro. **(D)** violates Rule 3 by having no photographs by Hue in Lifestyle, but one photograph by Fuentes in Sports. **(A)** violates Rule 4 by including a photograph by Gagnon in Sports. That leaves **(B)** as the correct answer.

8. (C) "If" / Must Be True

For this question, both photos in the Lifestyle section will be by Hue—that's Option III. If you didn't do Limited Options, you'd simply create a new sketch with the new "if." With both photos in the Lifestyle section by Hue, that means both photos in the Sports section must be by Fuentes (Rule 3). Because Hue is the only photographer in Lifestyle, there must also be at least one photo by Hue in Metro (Rule 2). There is one photo left in Metro, which must be assigned to Gagnon because per Rule 1 each photographer must be assigned at least once.

Lif	Met	Spo
H	H	F
H	G	F

With only one photo by Gagnon, **(C)** is the correct answer.

9. (D) "If" / Must Be True

For this question, Lifestyle will have one photo by Gagnon and the other by Hue—that's Option II. If you didn't set up Limited Options, just set up a new sketch incorporating the new "if." Because only one Lifestyle photo is by Hue, there must be just one photo in Sports by Fuentes (Rule 3). The second photo in Sports cannot be by Gagnon (Rule 4), so it must be by Hue. Because Gagnon and Hue are the photographers assigned to Lifestyle, at least one of them must also be assigned to Metro (Rule 2). The second photo in Metro could be by any of the photographers.

Lif	Met	Spo
H	G/H	F
G		H

There must be just one photo by Hue in Sports, making **(D)** the correct answer. **(A)**, **(B)**, and **(C)** *could* be true, but need not be. **(E)** must be false.

10. (A) Could Be True

The correct answer to this question will be an acceptable set of assignments for Fuentes. The four wrong answers will all be impossible.

If Fuentes had one photo in each section, the second photo in each section would have to be by Gagnon or Hue. With one photo by Fuentes in Sports, Hue would have to have one photo in Lifestyle (Rule 3). Gagnon cannot have a photo in Sports, so the second photo there would also have to be by Hue. Gagnon still has to be assigned at least once, so the second photo in Metro will be by Gagnon.

Lif	Met	Spo
F	F	F
H	G	H

This is acceptable, making **(A)** the correct answer. Fortunately, the correct answer was right at the top. Test takers could have saved time by temporarily skipping this question and drawing a sketch for the next question. The sketch for the next question allows for this very scenario and could have been used to verify this answer immediately.

As for the wrong answers: if there were two photos by Fuentes in the Sports section, there would also have to be two photos by Hue in the Lifestyle section (Rule 3), making **(B)** impossible because it has a photo by Fuentes in Sport.

As for **(D)**, those two photos by Fuentes in the Sports section would again force two of Hue's photos into the Lifestyle section (Rule 3), and this time there is room for them. However, because Hue is the only photographer in the Lifestyle section, there also must be a photo by Hue in the Metro section (Rule 2), and the final photo in Metro would have to be by Gagnon, who hasn't been assigned yet. **(D)**, however, also has a photo by Fuentes in the Metro section, creating three photos there, which is impossible.

If there were one photo by Fuentes in the Sports section, there would have to be a photo by Hue in the Lifestyle section (Rule 3), making **(C)** impossible because it has the Lifestyle section filled with two photos by Fuentes.

In **(E)**, Fuentes has one photo in the Sports section and can still be assigned two more times. However, in this case, Fuentes could not be assigned both photos in Metro because that would leave only Hue and Gagnon in Lifestyle, with no common photographer between Lifestyle and Metro, violating Rule 2. That means **(E)** is impossible.

11. (C) "If" / Could Be True

For this question, the two photos in Lifestyle are assigned to Fuentes and Hue—Option II. With Hue assigned to just one photo in Lifestyle, there must be just one photo in Sports by Fuentes (Rule 3). The second photo in Sports cannot be by Gagnon (Rule 4), so it must be by Hue. Gagnon still has to be assigned at least once, so one of the photos in Metro must be by Gagnon. The second Metro photo must be by one of the photographers assigned to Lifestyle (Rule 2), which means it will be by either Fuentes or Hue.

Lif	Met	Spo
F	G	F
H	F/H	H

Hue could have a photo in Metro, making **(C)** the correct answer.

12. (E) "If" / Could Be True

For this question, one of the sections will have two photos by Gagnon. Gagnon cannot be assigned to Sports, so this could only happen in Lifestyle or Metro. Draw out both possibilities.

If there were two photos by Gagnon in Lifestyle, there would have to also be a photo by Gagnon in Metro (Rule 2). That's three photos for Gagnon, and that's all (Rule 1). With no photos by Hue in Lifestyle, there would be no photos by Fuentes in Sports (Rule 3), so the Sports photos must both be by Hue. Fuentes still needs to be assigned at least once, so Fuentes will be assigned the second photo in Metro.

Lif	Met	Spo
G	G	H
G	F	H

If there were two photos by Gagnon in Metro, there would have to be a photo by Gagnon in Lifestyle (Rule 2). That's Gagnon's maximum of three photos. The second photo in Lifestyle could be by Fuentes or Hue. As for Sports, both photos can't be by Fuentes because there aren't two photos by Hue in Lifestyle (Rule 3), so at least one photo in Sports will be by Hue. The other one will be by either Fuentes or Hue. Fuentes will have to have a photo in either the Lifestyle or Sports section (Rule 1).

Lif	Met	Spo
G	G	H
F/H	G	H/F

The first option here was enough to verify that both photos in Sports could be by Hue, making **(E)** the correct answer. The second option helps verify why the remaining answers all must be false.

13. (C) "If" / Could Be True

For this question, the two photos in Metro will be by Fuentes and Hue. Gagnon still needs to be assigned, and cannot be assigned to Sports (Rule 4). With Metro filled up, Gagnon must be assigned a photo in Lifestyle. The second photo in Lifestyle must be assigned to someone assigned to Metro (Rule 2), so it will be either Fuentes or Hue.

Lif	Met	Spo
G	F	
F/H	H	

If the second photo in Lifestyle is by Fuentes, there would be no photos by Hue in Lifestyle. That would mean no photos by

Fuentes in Sports (Rule 3), so both Sports photos would be by Hue.

Lif	Met	Spo
G	F	H
F	H	H

If the second photo in Lifestyle is by Hue, there would be one photo by Hue in Lifestyle. That would mean exactly one photo by Fuentes in Sports (Rule 2). The other Sports photo would have to be by Hue.

Lif	Met	Spo
G	F	F
H	H	H

In that second option, Lifestyle could have photos by Gagnon and Hue, making **(C)** the correct answer. The remaining answers all must be false.

Game 3: Campus Art Gallery

Step 1: Overview

Situation: Students working shifts at an art gallery exhibit

Entities: Five students (Grecia, Hakeem, Joe, Katya, Louise)

Action: Strict Sequencing. Determine the schedule, in order from Monday to Friday, for the five students.

Limitations: Each day will include 2 shifts (first and second) for a total of 10 shifts. The shifts are "nonoverlapping," so they are distinct. Each student will be assigned to exactly two of those shifts. Each shift is worked by just one student, so there is no sharing of shifts.

Step 2: Sketch

The idea of multiple shifts may seem intimidating. However, there's not much going on here that's different from any standard Sequencing game. Set up the order from Monday to Friday, but just place *two* spaces under each day. Draw them one on top of the other so that there's a distinct row for each shift (rather than a consecutive line of 10 slots with the first and second shift alternating between slots). Because each student will be used twice, list two of each by initial:

```
        G G H H J J K K L L

        Mo  Tu  We  Th  Fr
    1: ___ ___ ___ ___ ___
    2: ___ ___ ___ ___ ___
```

Step 3: Rules

Rule 1 prevents any student from working two shifts on the same day. Make a shorthand note to the side ("Never 2 shifts same day"), or draw a block using the letter "X" as a variable, like so:

$$\boxed{\genfrac{}{}{0pt}{}{\cancel{X}}{X}}$$

Rule 2 creates a Block of Entities. Louise will work on two consecutive days:

$$\boxed{LL}$$

Both shifts will be the second shift, so draw this block next to the bottom row of the sketch.

Rule 3 states that both of Grecia's shifts will be the first shift. Furthermore, they *cannot* be consecutive. Next to the top row of the sketch, draw two Gs. To represent them being nonconsecutive, add a note to the side: "No GG."

Or, draw the Gs with at least one space in between, with an ellipsis to indicate the possibility of more spaces:

$$G\_\_\ ...\ G$$

Rule 4 assigns Katya to Tuesday and Friday, but with no indication of which shift on either day. So, draw a K under each day.

Rule 5 creates a Block of Entities with Hakeem and Joe. They must work together at least one day. They *could* work together

twice, but do not have to. Note that when they *do* work together, this rule does not indicate who works the first shift and who works the second. When you draw the block, you can draw both possibilities, like so:

$$\boxed{\genfrac{}{}{0pt}{}{H}{J}}\ or\ \boxed{\genfrac{}{}{0pt}{}{J}{H}}\quad \text{at least once}$$

Or you can use slash notation, like so:

$$\boxed{\genfrac{}{}{0pt}{}{H/J}{J/H}}\quad \text{at least once}$$

Rule 6 prevents Grecia and Louise from working together on any day.

$$\boxed{\genfrac{}{}{0pt}{}{\cancel{G}}{L}}\quad\boxed{\genfrac{}{}{0pt}{}{L}{\cancel{G}}}$$

Step 4: Deductions

There's a lot going on in this game, and investing in some good deductions really pays off in the questions. There is one Block of Entities that needs to appear: Hakeem and Joe (Rule 5). With Katya already working on Tuesday and Friday, Hakeem and Joe can only work together on Monday, Wednesday, or Thursday.

By itself, that's not information for Limited Options. However, the key issue in this game involves two very important Duplications: Grecia and Louise. They never work on the same day as one another. And, because nobody can work two shifts in one day (Rule 1), Grecia and Louise will work on four completely different days. None of those days will include Hakeem *and* Joe, so those two can only be together on whatever day is left. Knowing that Louise's days must be consecutive and Grecia's days *can't* be, the placement of Hakeem and Joe will be significant. Time to consider Limited Options.

If Hakeem and Joe were together on Monday, that would leave Tuesday through Friday for Grecia and Louise. Louise couldn't work Tuesday and Wednesday, otherwise Grecia would work consecutive shifts on Thursday and Friday. Similarly, Louise couldn't work Thursday and Friday, otherwise Grecia would work consecutive shifts on Tuesday and Wednesday. So, the only way this works is if Louise works Wednesday and Thursday, with Grecia working on Tuesday and Friday. Grecia works the first shift on her days, and Louise works the second shift on her days. With Grecia working the first shift on Tuesday and Friday, Katya must work the second shifts on those days (Rule 4). The first shifts on Wednesday and Thursday would be by Hakeem and Joe, in either order.

```
I)      Mo   Tu   We   Th   Fr
   1:   J/H   G   J/H  H/J   G
   2:   H/J   K    L    L    K
```

If Hakeem and Joe were together on Wednesday, Louise would work Monday and Tuesday or Thursday and Friday. However, if Louise worked Monday and Tuesday, Grecia would be left with consecutive days Thursday and Friday. If Louise worked Thursday and Friday, Grecia would again be left with consecutive days Monday and Tuesday. Either way, Rule 3 would be violated, making this option impossible.

So, the only other option is to put Hakeem and Joe on Thursday. In that case, Louise's consecutive shifts would have to be on either Monday and Tuesday or Tuesday and Wednesday. Either way, Louise will be on Tuesday's second shift (Rule 2)—along with Katya (Rule 4), who will then take the first shift. One of Grecia's shifts will be the day Louise does *not* work (Monday or Wednesday). Her second shift will have to be the only day left: Friday. She'll take the first shift (Rule 3), and Katya will be on Friday with her (Rule 4) in the second shift.

```
II)   Mo  Tu  We  Th  Fr
 1:  ___  K  ___  J/H  G
 2:  ___  L  ___  H/J  K
```

Step 5: Questions

14. (A) Partial Acceptability

The correct answer here will be acceptable—the one answer that doesn't violate any rules. However, the answers only list the second shift. Start by testing the rules one at a time, eliminating answers that violate those rules. With any remaining answers, consider who would be assigned the first shift, then test those answers to the rules.

Without seeing the first shift, Rule 1 cannot be tested. **(C)** violates Rule 2 by having Louise work only one second shift. **(D)** also violates Rule 2 by having Louise work shifts that are not consecutive. **(B)** violates Rule 3 by having Grecia work a second shift. The remaining rules cannot be tested without knowing who works the first shift.

With **(A)**, Louise is assigned Tuesday and Wednesday. Katya would be the first shift on Tuesday (Rule 4). Grecia cannot be assigned Tuesday or Wednesday (Rule 6) and cannot be assigned to both Thursday and Friday (Rule 3). So, Grecia would have to be assigned Monday and one other day. Hakeem and Joe would have to work one day together, so that would have to happen on Thursday. Grecia's second day would then be Friday, leaving Joe to round out the schedule on Wednesday.

```
A)   Mo  Tu  We  Th  Fr
 1:   G   K   J   J   G
 2:   H   L   L   H   K
```

That is acceptable, making **(A)** the correct answer. For the record:

(E) has Louise working Monday and Tuesday. Grecia could not work those days (Rule 6). Because she cannot work consecutive days, she would have to work Wednesday and Friday. However, this answer would then have Grecia on Friday with Joe, violating Rule 4 by leaving no room for Katya.

```
E)   Mo  Tu  We  Th  F̶r̶
 1:  ___  K   G  ___  G
 2:   L   L   H   J   J
                        K?
```

15. (C) Must Be True

The correct answer to this question must be true. The remaining answers could be true, but could also be false.

Limited Options makes short work of this question. In the first option, Grecia *could* work on Tuesday, Hakeem *could* work on Wednesday, and Joe *could* work on Thursday. That means **(A)**, **(B)**, and **(D)** all could be false. As for **(E)**, although Louise does not work on Tuesday in the first option, in the second option, she *does* work on Tuesday, which means **(E)** could be false. That leaves **(C)**, which must be true—Joe is never on Tuesday.

This could also be handled deftly without Limited Options. Temporarily skip this question, and use sketches drawn for later "if" questions. The sketches eventually lead to the same options, allowing for equally effective elimination.

As final proof, Joe cannot work on Tuesday because then Joe would work with Katya (Rule 4). With Tuesday filled up, Louise and Grecia would have to be each assigned to one of the other four days (Rule 6). But that would leave no day to have Joe and Hakeem together, violating Rule 5.

16. (B) "If" / Must Be True

For this question, Hakeem will work on Wednesday. That cannot be the same day as Joe. Otherwise, Wednesday would be filled. Then, Louise would have to be on consecutive days, Monday and Tuesday or Thursday and Friday. But that would force Grecia to be on the other two consecutive days, violating Rule 3. With Katya already working on Tuesday and Friday (Rule 4), Hakeem and Joe can only work together on Monday or Thursday, as already outlined in the Limited Options in Step 4.

For this question, Hakeem will be the first shift on Wednesday, making Joe take the first shift on Thursday in the first option.

```
I)   Mo  Tu  We  Th  Fr
 1:  J/H  G   H   J   G
 2:  H/J  K   L   L   K
```

In the second option, Hakeem could be with Grecia or Louise on Wednesday. Either way, Joe's second shift would have to occur on Monday, with either Grecia or Louise.

```
II)   Mo  Tu  We  Th  Fr
 1:  ___  K  ___  J/H  G
 2:  ___  L  ___  H/J  K
       J        H
      L/G      G/L
```

In either case, Joe always works on Monday and Thursday, making **(B)** the correct answer.

17. (E) "If" / Could Be True

For this question, Grecia and Joe have to work together one day. It couldn't be on Tuesday or Friday because Katya works those days (Rule 4). That leaves Monday, Wednesday, or Thursday. There also has to be a day with Hakeem and Joe (Rule 5). As outlined in Step 4, Hakeem and Joe could only be together on Monday or Thursday. If they were together on Monday, Louise would have to be on Wednesday and Thursday so that Grecia's shifts could be split between Tuesday and Friday. However, that would force Grecia to be with Katya both days and never with Joe. So, that option cannot apply here.

That means only the second option applies, with Hakeem and Joe on Thursday. That means Grecia could be with Joe on either Monday or Wednesday. Test them both.

If Grecia and Joe were together on Monday, Grecia would be the first shift (Rule 3), putting Joe on the second shift. Louise's consecutive days would have to be Tuesday and Wednesday. Katya would be on Tuesday and Friday. Grecia's second shift would be on Friday, leaving Hakeem to work the first shift on Wednesday.

	Mo	Tu	We	Th	Fr
1:	G	K	H	J/H	G
2:	J	L	L	H/J	K

If Grecia and Joe were together on Wednesday, Grecia would be the first shift (Rule 3), putting Joe on the second shift. Louise's consecutive days would have to be Monday and Tuesday. Katya would be on Tuesday and Friday. Grecia's second shift would be on Friday, leaving Hakeem to work the first shift on Monday.

	Mo	Tu	We	Th	Fr
1:	H	K	G	J/H	G
2:	L	L	J	H/J	K

Either way, Joe would be on Thursday and could work either shift that day. That makes **(E)** the correct answer. For the record, **(A)** is impossible because Grecia is not on Tuesday in either case. The remaining answers list possible *days* for each student, but Hakeem can only work the *first* shift on Monday or Wednesday, and Joe can only work the *second* shift on Wednesday.

18. (B) "If" / Could Be True

For this question, Katya works the *second* shift on Tuesday—that's only possible in Option I. Using that option, only **(B)** is possible, making it the correct answer. The other answer choices all must be false. Check back in Step 4 to see the deductions that led to Option I if necessary.

Game 4: Publishing Cookbooks

Step 1: Overview

Situation: A publisher scheduling the release of six cookbooks

Entities: Six cookbooks (K, L, M, N, O, P) and two seasons (fall and spring)

Action: Distribution. Determine in which season each cookbook will be published.

Limitations: Each cookbook will be published in just one season. There's no minimum or maximum number of cookbooks for each season.

Step 2: Sketch

List the cookbooks. Then, set up a chart with two columns: one for fall and one for spring. Because there's no minimum or maximum number of cookbooks in each season, leave the columns empty for now.

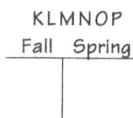

$$\text{KLMNOP}$$
$$\text{Fall} \quad \text{Spring}$$

Step 3: Rules

Rule 1 prevents M and P from being published in the same season. That means one will be published in the fall and the other in the spring. Set up a slot in each column and enter "M/P" in each slot.

Rule 2 creates a Block of Entities with K and N. They could go in either season, so draw the block to the side.

$$\frac{K}{N}$$

Rule 3 introduces some Formal Logic. If K is published in the fall, then O is published in the fall. By contrapositive, if O is published in the spring (i.e., *not* in fall), then K must be published in the spring (i.e., *not* in fall):

$$\frac{\text{Fall}}{K} \rightarrow \frac{\text{Fall}}{O}$$

$$\frac{\text{Spring}}{O} \rightarrow \frac{\text{Spring}}{K}$$

Note that this does *not* mean that K and O have to be published in the same season. If K is published in the spring, it's not certain that O is published then, too. It's perfectly acceptable for K to be published in the spring while O is published in the fall.

Rule 4 is more Formal Logic. If M is published in the fall, then N must be published in the spring. By contrapositive, if N is published in the fall (i.e., *not* in spring), then M must be published in the spring (i.e., *not* in fall):

$$\frac{\text{Fall}}{M} \rightarrow \frac{\text{Spring}}{N}$$

$$\frac{\text{Fall}}{N} \rightarrow \frac{\text{Spring}}{M}$$

Note that this does *not* mean that M and N are published in different seasons. They cannot be both published in the fall—publishing either one in the fall results in the other being published in the spring. However, if either one is published in the spring, then the logic dictates nothing. It's possible that both are published in the spring.

Step 4: Deductions

The block of K and N allows for Limited Options. In the first option, K and N would be published in fall. In that case, with K in the fall, O would also be in the fall (Rule 3). And with N in the fall, M would have to be in the spring (contrapositive of Rule 4). With M in the spring, P would have to be in the fall (Rule 1). That leaves L, which is unrestricted by the rules (i.e., a Floater). L could be published in either season.

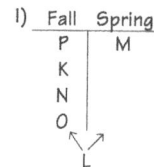

I)
Fall	Spring
P	M
K	
N	
O	

L

In the second option, K and N would be published in the fall. In that case, neither piece of Formal Logic is triggered. So, M and P could still be published in either order. O could now be published in either season without violating the rules. And L is still a Floater, so L could also be published in either season.

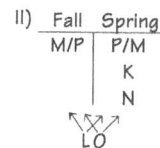

II)
Fall	Spring
M/P	P/M
	K
	N

L O

Limited Options could also be set up using the first rule. If M were published in the fall, P would be published in the spring. With M in the fall, N would be there, too. That would bring along K. With K in the fall, O would be there, too. L would be a Floater and could be published in either season. If M were published in the spring, P would be published in the fall. However, that's as far as that option would go.

Either way, Limited Options are great but hardly necessary in this game. The biggest key is to avoid mistranslating Rules 3 and 4. As long as you stay consistent to the logic, the questions can be readily handled with or without Limited Options.

Step 5: Questions

19. (E) Acceptability

As with all Acceptability questions, go through the rules one at a time, eliminating answers that violate those rules.

(B) violates Rule 1 by having M and P in the same season. **(A)** violates Rule 2 by having K and N in different seasons. **(C)** violates Rule 3 by having K in the fall, then putting O in the spring. **(D)** violates Rule 4 by having M in the fall, then putting N also in the fall. That leaves **(E)** as the correct answer.

20. (C) "If" / Could Be True

For this question, M is published in the fall. That means P is published in the spring (Rule 1). With M in the fall, N must also be published in the spring (Rule 4). N must be published with K (Rule 2), so K will be in the spring.

Fall	Spring
M	P
	N
	K

With P, N, and K in the spring, any answer containing any of those cookbooks must be false. That eliminates **(A)**, **(B)**, **(D)**, and **(E)**—leaving **(C)** as the right answer. Both L and O *could* be in the fall.

21. (B) "If" / Could Be True

For this question, N will be published in the fall. That only happens in Option I of the Limited Options set up in Step 4. The question can still be handled quickly even without the Limited Options. If N is in the fall, K will be published in the fall, too (Rule 2). Also, with N published in the fall, M couldn't be in the fall (Rule 4), so M would be published in the spring. That would mean P is published in the fall (Rule 1). Finally, with K in the fall, O must be there, too (Rule 3). That leaves L, which is entirely unrestricted and could be published in either season.

Fall	Spring
N	M
K	
P	
O	

The fastest path to the right answer for a "Could Be True" question in a game that contains a Floater may be to consider any answer about the Floater right away. L is never restricted by the rules, so it could always go in either season. That makes **(B)** the correct answer.

22. (A) Completely Determine

The correct answer to this question will make it possible to determine in which season every cookbook is published for certain. The remaining answers will all allow for some uncertainty. Given that L is a Floater, it will need to be nailed down, and four of the answer choices do just that. Also,

answers that trigger a Formal Logic rule are more likely to be correct.

If K is published in the fall, then so is N (Rule 2) and so is O (Rule 3). With N published in the fall, M would have to be published in the spring (Rule 4), which would mean P is published in the fall (Rule 1). Publishing L in the spring would make every cookbook scheduled.

Fall	Spring
K	L
N	M
O	
P	

That makes **(A)** the correct answer. For the record:

No matter when O and P are published, it would not be possible to determine in which season L is published. That eliminates **(B)**.

If P is published in the fall, then M is published in the spring (Rule 1). However, N and K could still be published in either season, no matter when L is published. That eliminates **(C)**.

If K is published in the spring, then so is N (Rule 3). However, that doesn't help determine in which seasons M and P are published, no matter when L is published. That eliminates **(D)**.

If M is published in the fall, then P is published in the spring (Rule 1) and N is published in the spring (Rule 4). If N is published in the spring, so is K (Rule 2). However, even placing L in the fall does nothing to confirm in which season O is published. That eliminates **(E)**.

Fall	Spring
M	P
L	N
	K

O

23. (B) Rule Substitution

For this question, Rule 4 is removed from the game. The correct answer will be a rule that could replace Rule 4 without changing anything from the original setup. In other words, it will reestablish the original rule without adding any new restrictions.

L was never involved in any of the original rules, so adding a condition based on when L is published would change the game. That eliminates **(A)**.

(B) tries a different piece of Formal Logic. If N is published in the fall, then so is P. By Rule 1, that would mean M is published in the spring. So, the effect of this rule would be: If N is published in the fall, then M is published in the spring. By contrapositive, if M is published in the fall (i.e., *not* the spring), then N would have to be published in the spring (i.e., *not* the fall). That's an exact replacement for Rule 4, making this the correct answer. For the record:

(C) states that publishing M in the spring would place P in the fall, which would always happen by Rule 1. However, that makes no connection between M and N, so this would not help replace Rule 4.

(D) contradicts the original rule that was removed. By this logic, if N is published in the spring, then so is M. However, the contrapositive of this says that if M is published in the fall (i.e., *not* the spring), then N must be in the fall (i.e., *not* the spring). That's the exact opposite of the original rule.

(E) is valid by the original rules. If O is published in the spring, then so is K (Rule 3), which means so is N (Rule 2). However, this makes no connection between M and N, so it does not help replace Rule 4.

Section IV: Logical Reasoning

Q#	Question Type	Correct	Difficulty
1	Assumption (Sufficient)	C	★
2	Principle (Identify/Assumption)	B	★
3	Paradox	D	★
4	Point at Issue	B	★
5	Flaw	C	★
6	Parallel Flaw	D	★
7	Role of a Statement	C	★
8	Strengthen	E	★
9	Principle (Identify/Inference)	C	★★
10	Point at Issue	E	★★
11	Principle (Apply/Inference)	B	★
12	Assumption (Necessary)	B	★★★
13	Flaw	D	★★
14	Assumption (Sufficient)	B	★
15	Flaw	D	★
16	Assumption (Necessary)	B	★★
17	Inference	A	★★
18	Assumption (Necessary)	E	★★★★
19	Inference	A	★★★
20	Assumption (Necessary)	C	★★
21	Weaken	C	★★★★
22	Parallel Reasoning	A	★★★★
23	Weaken	D	★★★
24	Assumption (Necessary)	D	★★★
25	Paradox	C	★★★

1. (C) Assumption (Sufficient)

Step 1: Identify the Question Type

The question asks for something that makes the argument valid "if … assumed," making this a Sufficient Assumption question.

Step 2: Untangle the Stimulus

Aisha states that Vadim will be laid off. Despite his excellent programming skills, the firm is laying off a programmer, which always involves laying off the programmer hired most recently.

Step 3: Make a Prediction

There's no evidence that Vadim is the most recently hired programmer. But if he is, then he would definitely be the first person laid off according to the company policy, ensuring Aisha's argument is correct.

Step 4: Evaluate the Answer Choices

(C) is correct, making Aisha's argument complete.

(A) is a Distortion. The layoff is based on how long programmers have worked *at the firm*. Experience can involve earlier work at other companies, which is surely not considered in this decision.

(B) is Out of Scope. The decision is made purely on what policy dictates, regardless of how clearly it was explained.

(D) is irrelevant. Vadim's work has been exemplary, but maybe he's still the worst of the bunch. However, the quality of the work doesn't matter. The decision is based on who was hired most recently.

(E) is Out of Scope. The argument is not about whether the policy is good or bad. It's about whether the policy applies to Vadim, which it only does if he's the most recently hired programmer.

2. (B) Principle (Identify/Assumption)

Step 1: Identify the Question Type

The correct answer will be a principle *underlying* the response, making this an Identify the Principle question that acts like an Assumption question.

Step 2: Untangle the Stimulus

As an artist, Wanda values visual stimuli in her work area. She likens herself to a writer who values written stimuli. Vernon accepts the analogy, but says there's a catch: writers value *good* writing as stimuli, not tabloids. He then questions Wanda's visual stimuli of laundry and garbage.

Step 3: Make a Prediction

Vernon is okay with an artist having stimuli, but doesn't feel that junk qualifies. Vernon is acting on the principle that proper artistic stimuli should at least be *good* stimuli.

Step 4: Evaluate the Answer Choices

(B) gets to Vernon's concern. If quality matters, then laundry piles and empty glass bottles are certainly as questionable as Vernon suggests.

(A) is Out of Scope. Vernon is not concerned with Wanda's *health*, but rather her ability to be inspired by the clutter around her.

(C) is too specific. Vernon definitely suggests that tabloids are inferior to "good writing." However, tabloids have nothing to do with Wanda's circumstance, so a principle about them would not pertain.

(D) is a Distortion. Vernon is not so much concerned about the messiness itself. If the mess contained something appropriately stimulating as opposed to laundry and garbage, Vernon might accept the mess.

(E) is a Distortion. Vernon's unhappiness with Wanda's choice of stimuli doesn't mean he encourages working in an empty area. He just wants Wanda's stimuli to be less junk and more *good* stuff.

3. (D) Paradox

Step 1: Identify the Question Type

The question asks for something that will "account for" the given results. That suggests that the results are not what one would expect, making this a Paradox question.

Step 2: Untangle the Stimulus

Although designating an animal as *endangered* leads to greater legal protection of that animal, many animals start to disappear even *more* quickly after they're listed as endangered.

Step 3: Make a Prediction

For Paradox questions, always ask "why." In this case, why are endangered animals dying out more quickly when being labeled as endangered gives them legal protection? Something must happen to these animals after they're placed on the endangered list. The correct answer will describe something that makes them more vulnerable.

Step 4: Evaluate the Answer Choices

(D) helps resolve the mystery. Calling animals *endangered* makes them more desirable to collectors, who will be more eager to find and collect that rare species before it disappears forever.

(A) is Out of Scope. The increased rate of disappearance only occurs *after* the animal is listed. It doesn't matter how long it takes for that official listing to take place.

(B) doesn't help. Even though some endangered animals may not get enough affection to warrant a public campaign, they would still be subject to stricter laws and restrictions. Their rapid decline is still a mystery.

(C) doesn't help. No matter how many animals are listed, laws and restrictions should still protect them, or at least not exacerbate their diminished numbers.

(E) is a 180. If endangered animals become harder to find and poach, then it's even *more* unusual that they're dying off more quickly.

4. (B) Point at Issue

Step 1: Identify the Question Type

There are two speakers, and the question asks for a point over which they *disagree*. That makes this a Point at Issue question.

Step 2: Untangle the Stimulus

Sefu wants the town council to adopt his development plan. Annette recommends Sefu take the council to other towns that have successfully adopted the same plan. Sefu is hesitant because the vote affects him directly and he wants to avoid the appearance of impropriety.

Step 3: Make a Prediction

Sefu probably agrees that taking the council to other towns would help sell the development plan. However, the question is whether he *should*. Annette says he should, but Sefu feels otherwise. That's the point at issue.

Step 4: Evaluate the Answer Choices

(B) is correct. Using the Decision Tree, Annette has an opinion about this (she says he *should*), and Sefu has an opinion (he implies he *shouldn't*). And they do disagree.

(A) is a 180. Sefu and Annette both seem to want the development plan to succeed. They disagree over the idea of aiding that success by taking the council on a trip.

(C) is not a contentious point. Only Sefu mentions his having a vested interest. Annette makes no mention of that and accordingly has no opinion about it.

(D) is a 180. Annette brings this point up directly, but Sefu doesn't dispute it. The problem Sefu has is taking the council *himself* to see those success stories.

(E) is definitely something Sefu advocates. However, Annette never addresses it. It's possible that she would agree, but wasn't aware of that issue until Sefu brought it up.

5. (C) Flaw

Step 1: Identify the Question Type

The question directly asks why the argument is flawed. However, the question provides some extra assistance, stating that the answer is something the scholar "presumes

without giving sufficient justification." In other words, the answer will express an unwarranted assumption.

Step 2: Untangle the Stimulus

As some religions have adapted to modern times, worship attendance for those religions has increased. The scholar concludes that other religions will see the same results if they also keep up with the times.

Step 3: Make a Prediction

This is a classic error of Causation versus Correlation. While it's a remarkable coincidence that worship increased just after the modern updates, there's still no evidence that those updates were definitely the *cause* of the attendance increase. The scholar mistakenly assumes as much, as the correct answer should mention.

Step 4: Evaluate the Answer Choices

(C) is exactly the causal assumption made by the scholar.

(A) is not suggested. The scholar concludes that the attendance will increase for any religion that *can* modernize, but never suggests or assumes that there are religions that *can't*.

(B) is Out of Scope. The argument only connects modernization to attendance. Whether the message changes or not has no effect on the argument.

(D) is Extreme. The scholar concludes that modernization guarantees increased attendance, but never implies it is the *only* way to do so.

(E) is Extreme. The attendance increase does not have to be *irreversible*. As long as the increase occurs at all, the scholar's argument stands.

6. (D) Parallel Flaw

Step 1: Identify the Question Type

The correct answer will be an argument that "most closely resembles" the one in the stimulus. Furthermore, the reasoning in both arguments will be *flawed*, making this a Parallel Flaw question. Be sure to find the answer that commits the exact same logical flaw as the stimulus argument.

Step 2: Untangle the Stimulus

Being in the regional band requires a lot of practice or great talent. Lily is in the regional band and is talented, so the author concludes she doesn't really practice.

Step 3: Make a Prediction

Participation in the band requires *at least* one of two qualities: practice or talent. The word *or* is inclusive and allows the possibility of *both*. In other words, it's possible that participants could practice hard *and* be talented. The author makes it exclusive (i.e., you can only do one or the other, not both), and there's no logical basis for that. The correct answer will similarly provide two possible requirements and then suggest that meeting one excludes the possibility of meeting the other.

Step 4: Evaluate the Answer Choices

(D) is a match. There are two possible requirements (to stay informed, one must read the newspaper or watch the news on TV), and the author suggests that meeting one (informed Julie reads the paper) means not meeting the other (she doesn't watch TV news).

(A) only lists one requirement (good weather), so it cannot make the same inclusive/exclusive error.

(B) does provide two requirements (Chicago or Toronto) for going on vacation, but Lois doesn't actually go on vacation. Thus, the requirements are irrelevant, and the logic doesn't match.

(C) is a Distortion. "Neither … nor" means "not one… *and* not the other." So, the requirement for Johnson is that Horan doesn't run *and* Jacobs doesn't run. That's not the same "one or the other" requirement from the stimulus. And while the logic *is* flawed (classic Necessity vs. Sufficiency), it's not the *same* flaw as the original.

(E) is a Distortion. There are two possible requirements, but this argument says that *not* meeting one requires meeting the other—the opposite of the stimulus. Moreover, there's no indication that Wayne definitely gets a ride home, so the requirements are irrelevant anyway.

7. (C) Role of a Statement

Step 1: Identify the Question Type

The question provides a claim from the stimulus and asks for its *role* in the argument, making this a Role of a Statement question. Start by locating the claim in question, which in this case is the very last sentence of the argument. Then, break the argument into evidence and conclusion, and determine why the dietitian included that final claim.

Step 2: Untangle the Stimulus

The dietitian argues that eating fish can lower one's cholesterol. The evidence involves a study of two groups, one that ate fish and one that didn't. After the study, the people who ate fish had lower cholesterol than the people who didn't. Before the study, the cholesterol level of each group was roughly the same.

Step 3: Make a Prediction

The direct evidence for the dietitian's claim is the lower cholesterol level *after* the study. So, why mention the cholesterol level *before* the study? Well, if the first group had lower levels to begin with, then nothing would have changed. The lower cholesterol would be a preexisting condition,

possibly caused by other factors. By citing the initial results, the dietitian eliminates that possibility and makes it more likely for the fish to be responsible.

Step 4: Evaluate the Answer Choices

(C) is correct. It rules out the possibility that the lower cholesterol levels were caused by something else *before* the study.

(A) is a 180. If the first group had lower levels to begin with, *that* would be an objection, suggesting an alternative possibility. However, the claim in question suggests the exact opposite.

(B) is inaccurate. The conclusion here is the very first sentence, not the claim in question.

(D) is Out of Scope. There is no background info on the *purpose* of this study.

(E) is a Distortion. The starting cholesterol levels do not explain why eating fish can lower those levels.

8. (E) Strengthen

Step 1: Identify the Question Type

The question directly asks for something that would strengthen the given argument.

Step 2: Untangle the Stimulus

The author is singing the praises of satnavs, concluding that they help save gas and increase safety. They give drivers shorter routes, which can reduce fuel usage. And drivers don't get distracted looking at maps.

Step 3: Make a Prediction

Satnavs clearly have a lot of advantages, but are there any disadvantages? The author assumes otherwise, or at least that any advantages are more significant than the disadvantages. To strengthen the argument, the correct answer will either eliminate a disadvantage or add yet another reason why satnavs are awesome.

Step 4: Evaluate the Answer Choices

(E) supports the author's claim. If people take fewer risks, that bolsters the claim that satnavs "promote safety."

(A) is an Irrelevant Comparison. It doesn't matter who uses satnavs more frequently. What matters is whether or not satnavs are better for safety and fuel usage.

(B) offers no help. This explains *why* people would want to find a shorter route, but does nothing to support the idea that satnavs are a safer and more fuel-efficient solution.

(C) is irrelevant. It doesn't matter how *likely* people are to use satnavs. The argument is whether satnavs help when they *are* used.

(D) is irrelevant and a 180 at worst. The argument is about how satnavs can help when they *are* used. If anything, this just suggests people ignore satnavs anyway, so they don't even get the chance to help.

9. (C) Principle (Identify/Inference)

Step 1: Identify the Question Type

The question asks for a *proposition* illustrated by the stimulus. That makes this an Identify the Principle question, and the principle will be inferred by broadening the scope of the situation described.

Step 2: Untangle the Stimulus

Managers should encourage employees to do their best, but threats and rewards aren't good enough. Employees have to *want* to do their best. So, the author recommends that managers give away some of their responsibilities to provide employees with the most effective motivation.

Step 3: Make a Prediction

The specific solution for the managers is to give up some responsibilities to employees so that the managers can better motivate the employees. The correct answer will describe this sacrificial act in more general terms.

Step 4: Evaluate the Answer Choices

(C) matches the idea. By partially relinquishing control (i.e., passing off responsibilities), managers can enhance their effectiveness as managers (i.e., better extract the best performance from employees).

(A) is a Distortion. Giving employees more responsibility is intended to increase their performance, not give them a better sense of "how power should be used."

(B) is Out of Scope. There's no mention of "prestige" or "job security."

(D) is Extreme. Giving more decision-making authority to employees doesn't mean they should be considered the *best* people to carry out those decisions. It just needs to encourage employees to perform their personal best.

(E) is Extreme. Harnessing self-interest (i.e., getting employees to *want* to do a good job) can help benefit managers, but that doesn't necessarily apply to the "company as a whole."

10. (E) Point at Issue

Step 1: Identify the Question Type

The question asks about two speakers and what they "disagree over," making this a Point at Issue question.

Step 2: Untangle the Stimulus

Richard argues that abstract art fails to represent anything, meaning it's not actually "art." He concludes that others will eventually agree. Jung-Su refutes this by saying that abstract art *does* represent, just not in a literal sense. Abstract art defies everyday perspectives and only represents the "formal features" of objects. Thus, it *is* art.

Step 3: Make a Prediction

The debate here focuses on whether abstract art qualifies as art or not, based on the requirement of representation. Richard says abstract art does *not* represent, so does *not* qualify as art. Jung-Su says the opposite. The correct answer will focus on this question of whether abstract art represents anything, thus qualifying it as art.

Step 4: Evaluate the Answer Choices

(E) is the point at issue. Richard has an opinion about this (it *fails* to be representational), as does Jung-Su (it *does* represent, but only formal features), and they certainly disagree.

(A) is a 180. Richard agrees with this, in that abstract art rejects *any* representation. But so does Jung-Su, who says that abstract art rejects "literal representation" in favor of a "purely formal" one. So, they agree about this.

(B) is stated by Richard, but Jung-Su does not dispute this requirement. The disagreement is over whether abstract art *meets* that requirement.

(C) is Out of Scope for Richard, who is only concerned with abstract art, not music.

(D) is stated by Richard. Jung-Su may hold the personal belief that it's *not* an aberration, but could still concede the point that it "will be seen as an aberration" by others.

11. (B) Principle (Apply/Inference)

Step 1: Identify the Question Type

The stimulus will contain *principles* that will be used to *justify* the correct answer. That means the general principle will be given, and you must apply the principle to the specific situation in the correct answer, which should conform to the same logic.

Step 2: Untangle the Stimulus

There are two principles. The first is that someone who intentionally brings about misfortune should be blamed for it. However, *some* people who bring about misfortune unintentionally should be free of blame. That brings up the second principle: if someone causes misfortune that couldn't be reasonably expected, that person should *not* be blamed.

Step 3: Make a Prediction

The first claim is absolute: if one *knows* there's going to be trouble, that person should be blamed. The key here is not to be fooled by the middle sentence. Only *some* people who unintentionally cause misfortune should be cleared of blame.

However, that allows for exceptions. The only situation that ensures being free from blame is if the misfortune was reasonably unforeseeable. If misfortune *is* foreseeable, the question of blame is open. Look for an answer in which someone acts *knowing* that misfortune will happen (making that person to blame) or in which someone acts with *no* reasonable expectation of misfortune (clearing the blame).

Step 4: Evaluate the Answer Choices

(B) is supported. While misfortune occurred (bankruptcy), Oblicek had no expectation and could not reasonably foresee that misfortune occurring. By the second principle, that frees Oblicek from blame.

(A) is a Distortion. Who knows why Riley was oblivious to the problem of parking in the middle of Main Street? However, an accident was entirely (and very reasonably) foreseeable, so the question of blame still looms.

(C) is a Distortion. Gougon was concerned, but he did not *know* his guests would become ill. While his decision was perhaps unwise, it's not enough to trigger the first principle and assign him blame.

(D) puts the blame on Dr. Fitzpatrick even though he did not *know* the blood pressure would go up. The fact that nobody else was involved is irrelevant to the first principle, which does not apply here.

(E) blames Kapp for the fire even though she didn't *know* it was going to happen. The first principle only states that people who *do* know are to blame.

12. (B) Assumption (Necessary)

Step 1: Identify the Question Type

The question asks for an *assumption* that the argument *requires*, making this a Necessary Assumption question.

Step 2: Untangle the Stimulus

The smell of lavender has been shown to reduce stress, and "intense stress" can make people more likely to get sick. Therefore, the researcher concludes that people who smell lavender regularly are less likely to get sick.

Step 3: Make a Prediction

Only "intense stress" is said to impair the immune system. Other stress levels, whether they be low, normal, or slightly high, may all have no effect on the immune system. So, regularly inhaling the scent of lavender would only help if it lowered stress down from *intense*. The researcher assumes that this is what happened.

Step 4: Evaluate the Answer Choices

(B) must be true. Some of these people *must* be highly stressed without the lavender. Otherwise, the lavender is not

reducing *intense* stress and thus could not be said to have any effect on the immune system.

(A) is Out of Scope. This argument is only about lavender. Whether or not other scents could help in other ways has no bearing on the argument.

(C) is an Irrelevant Comparison. It doesn't matter how these people's susceptibility compares to other people's. What matters is whether or not the lavender reduces their personal level of susceptibility.

(D) is not necessary. While the argument only mentions reducing stress, that doesn't imply that lavender can't have other, more significant effects that reduce susceptibility to illness.

(E) is a potential 180. It restricts the stress-relieving effect of lavender to just those people who experience intense stress. However, the first sentence of the stimulus says the scent of lavender can reduce stress generally. It's just those with intense stress that might get the decrease in susceptibility to disease, but anyone that smells it could get the stress-relief benefits.

13. (D) Flaw

Step 1: Identify the Question Type

The correct answer expresses why the argument is "vulnerable to criticism," which is a common LSAT phrase meaning the argument has a flaw.

Step 2: Untangle the Stimulus

Adjusting for inflation, the average family income increased over the past five years. The author concludes that the Andersen family's income increased because their income this year is average for families.

Step 3: Make a Prediction

The evidence is only about the Andersen family's income *this* year. What about their income five years ago? This argument only works if they maintained an average income. However, if their income was above average in the past, then they could have experienced a decrease. The author overlooks such a possibility.

Step 4: Evaluate the Answer Choices

(D) expresses the author's error.

(A) is not accurate. In both usages, *average* refers to the same statistical calculation.

(B) is not true. The conclusion refers to the family's "real income," which the author defines as "adjusted for inflation."

(C) is Out of Scope. The argument is only about the Andersen family. Even if most families' incomes are below average, the *average* income is still determined mathematically based on summing all the incomes and dividing them by the number of families—nothing requires an equal *number* of data points on either side of the average income value.

(E) is Extreme. While the author does assume that government statistics are reliable, that doesn't mean the government made *no* errors in gathering estimates.

14. (B) Assumption (Sufficient)

Step 1: Identify the Question Type

The correct answer will complete the argument *if* it were *assumed*, making this a Sufficient Assumption question.

Step 2: Untangle the Stimulus

Some counterfeiters carefully measure the images on real currency in order to make their counterfeit currency. Hence, the author concludes that images on banknotes *must* be difficult to measure accurately in order to stop counterfeiters.

Step 3: Make a Prediction

While creating difficult-to-measure images seems like a strong solution, it seems hasty to say this *must* be done. What if there are other actions that could just as easily prevent counterfeiting? The author is assuming that there are no viable alternatives, which is why prevention must involve difficult-to-measure images.

Step 4: Evaluate the Answer Choices

(B) is the assumption. This suggests that any other anti-counterfeiting method could be overcome by going back to accurately measured images. At that point, the counterfeiters cannot be stopped. So, no solution will work unless the images are, indeed, difficult to measure.

(A) is a 180. If copying technology is now this precise, then counterfeiters no longer need to measure anything, making the author's recommendation unnecessary.

(C) is a 180. If government has better printing technology, then an anti-counterfeiting solution need not involve hard-to-measure images. Instead, a solution can involve a complex printing pattern that only government printers can manage.

(D) suggests that there are many countries that *could* heed the author's advice. However, this still doesn't ensure that creating such images is necessary for counterfeit protection.

(E) does not guarantee the conclusion. Even if new designs can help minimize the *amount* of counterfeit currency, it still wouldn't entirely prevent it. What would entirely prevent it? There still could be several things that could be done, so **(E)** does not assure that difficult-to-measure images must be added.

15. (D) Flaw

Step 1: Identify the Question Type

The correct answer will point out why the argument is *flawed*, making this a Flaw question.

Step 2: Untangle the Stimulus

Dr. Sullivan advocates using nutritional supplements for a certain disease. However, Dr. Sullivan is getting paid to make that endorsement. Thus, Armstrong concludes that nutritional supplements should *not* be used.

Step 3: Make a Prediction

The problem is that Armstrong has no actual evidence against using nutritional supplements. By focusing exclusively on Dr. Sullivan's role as a paid spokesperson, Armstrong ignores any merit in Dr. Sullivan's claims.

Step 4: Evaluate the Answer Choices

(D) correctly expresses this ad hominem error of attacking the person making the argument rather than the argument itself.

(A) is not accurate. *Supplement* refers to the same kind of medication throughout the argument.

(B) is a 180. Armstrong is *rejecting* the voice of authority.

(C) is a Distortion. Armstrong does ignore the question of efficacy, but does not appeal to people's emotions. Instead, Armstrong appeals to questionable motives.

(E) is a Distortion. Armstrong doesn't assume that supplements *can't* be used in conjunction with other treatments (that would go against the very definition of a supplement). Armstrong merely argues that they *shouldn't* be used.

16. (B) Assumption (Necessary)

Step 1: Identify the Question Type

The question asks for an *assumption* that the argument *requires*, making this a Necessary Assumption question.

Step 2: Untangle the Stimulus

The economist is discussing the effects of a stronger economy. More parents will go back to work and need day care for their children. However, many day-care workers will quit to find better-paying jobs outside the day-care industry. According to the economist, this means finding day care will become more difficult for parents.

Step 3: Make a Prediction

There is a major overlooked possibility here. Sure, many day-care workers will look for new jobs. However, when one person quits, there may be plenty of other candidates ready to replace that person. The economist assumes otherwise, suggesting that nobody new will step in when the current day-care workers quit.

Step 4: Evaluate the Answer Choices

(B) must be true. The economist's argument hinges on day-care workers quitting and leaving an unfilled void. Using the Denial Test, if this *weren't* true, then there would be a host of new day-care workers, and the economist's argument is ruined.

(A) does not have to be true. Even if most new jobs *don't* pay well, there may still be enough well-paying jobs to lure day-care workers away.

(C) is a subtle Distortion. Even if day-care *centers* didn't lose workers, there could still be fewer independent day-care providers, fewer nannies, etc. In that case, the economist's argument still holds, so **(C)** does not have to be true.

(D) is a Distortion. While the economist implies that higher employment and departing day-care workers *will* lead to a shortage of day care, that doesn't mean day-care shortage couldn't happen under other conditions.

(E) is Out of Scope. The cost of day care is entirely unmentioned and irrelevant.

17. (A) Inference

Step 1: Identify the Question Type

The question asks for an answer "strongly supported" by the given *information*. That means the correct answer will be an inference.

Step 2: Untangle the Stimulus

According to the author, ostrich farming can be done on less land than cattle farming. Also, ostrich farming only requires two pairs of ostriches to start. Cattle farming requires a bull and an entire herd of cows. Starting an ostrich farm is more costly, but it can be more lucrative in the long run.

Step 3: Make a Prediction

It's impossible to predict exactly what the correct answer will say. However, it will be consistent with the facts about ostrich farming, including the need for less land, the smaller number of animals needed to start (even if they do cost more), and the considerably larger revenue it can produce.

Step 4: Evaluate the Answer Choices

(A) is supported. Two pairs of ostriches are needed to start up ostrich farming, and a herd of cows and a bull are needed to start up cattle farming. Land is also required, but less land is needed for ostriches than for cattle. So, because the author states that ostrich farming is more expensive to start up, it can be inferred that the four ostriches are more expensive than the herd of cows and a bull.

(B) is a Distortion. Ostrich farming may seem like a *better* source of income, but that doesn't mean cattle ranching is bad.

(C) is an Irrelevant Comparison. There's no information at all about food consumption.

(D) is a Distortion. Ostrich farming *can* bring in five times as much money, but that could be an upper limit, not the average. Even still, five times more income does not necessarily translate to five times more *profit*, which also has to factor in operational costs.

(E) is not supported. While the start-up costs may be expensive, it's possible that a bigger income is earned quickly enough to recoup those costs within a year.

18. (E) Assumption (Necessary)

Step 1: Identify the Question Type

The question asks for an *assumption* that the argument *requires*, making this a Necessary Assumption question.

Step 2: Untangle the Stimulus

This argument is about hairless dogs in Mexico and Peru. Hairlessness is too rare for these dogs to be unrelated (i.e., they didn't "emerge on two separate occasions"). However, there are no wild hairless dogs, and there's too much rough terrain between Mexico and Peru for them to have traveled over land. The author concludes that they *must* have gotten from one place to the other by boat.

Step 3: Make a Prediction

The argument focuses on how these related dogs got separated. The author rules out a couple of explanations. They don't have wild ancestors, so they didn't just migrate in different directions after evolving in the wild. And Mexico and Peru are separated by "mountainous jungle," so they probably didn't just walk themselves over from one country to the next. However, the author then decides they *must* have traveled from one place to the other by boat, overlooking any other explanation. The author assumes that no explanation other than "transported by boat" exists.

Step 4: Evaluate the Answer Choices

(E) must be true because it eliminates the likelihood of the dogs being transported a different way: over land. If this *weren't* true, and it was just as easy to travel over land, then trading expeditions could have taken dogs either way, negating the author's assertion that it *must* have been by boat.

(A) is not necessary. Even if such dogs are found elsewhere in the world, this doesn't address *how* they got from one place to the other. The author's argument still stands.

(B) is a Distortion. What's important is that any trade expeditions from *Peru* came by boat. Mexico could have done most of its trading over land with other countries, and the dogs still would have had to come from Peru by boat.

(C) is Extreme. The author merely claims that the dogs were *probably* transported during trading expeditions. That doesn't mean boats were never used for other purposes.

(D) is not necessary. The dogs didn't have to be traded themselves. They could have just hopped on the boats as stowaways or been given to people as gifts.

19. (A) Inference

Step 1: Identify the Question Type

The correct answer "must be true" based on what's given, making it an Inference question.

Step 2: Untangle the Stimulus

In Australia, researchers have found microdiamonds in the earth's crust that were formed 4.2 billion years ago, just 300 million years after the earth itself was formed.

Step 3: Make a Prediction

There are three dates to keep track of here. The earth formed 4.5 million years ago. Some microdiamonds formed in the crust 300 million years later. Present-day researchers found those microdiamonds. What happened in between those dates is unknown. Just stick to the timeline, and don't infer anything beyond what's known.

Step 4: Evaluate the Answer Choices

(A) is true. The crust *must* have started forming by that point because that's when the microdiamonds started forming there.

(B) does not have to be true. The microdiamonds are the earliest fragments "yet identified," but the crust could have started forming millions of years prior in any other part of the world.

(C) is not necessarily true. All that's known is that the crust was definitely forming, if not fully formed, by about 4.2 billion years ago. When it started to form and when it finished are unknown. It could have taken billions of years, or it could have taken just a couple of million.

(D) is not supported. They are described as the oldest fragments "yet identified," but that doesn't rule out the possibility of even older components that could be discovered in the future.

(E) is unsupported. The particular crystals discovered were formed 4.2 billion years ago, but there's nothing to suggest that there are no newer crystals that started forming eons after the crust was done forming.

20. (C) Assumption (Necessary)

Step 1: Identify the Question Type

The question asks for an *assumption* that is *required* by the argument, making this a Necessary Assumption question.

Step 2: Untangle the Stimulus

In the past, public squares provided an important forum for open discussion. Today, the Internet serves the same purpose, so the author concludes that the Internet should allow an equal amount of free expression.

Step 3: Make a Prediction

The issue here is one of Mismatched Concepts. The Internet is said to be replacing public squares as an open forum for discussion. However, the conclusion is that the Internet should have equal "freedom of expression." The author never mentions the role of free expression in public forums. For this argument to work, the author must assume that public forums depend upon that freedom of expression.

Step 4: Evaluate the Answer Choices

(C) must be assumed, claiming public forums would be less effective without free expression. Using the Denial Test, if forums could be *equally* effective without free expression, then the author's argument would be unsound.

(A) is Extreme. The author merely claims that the Internet should have "as much freedom of expression" as public squares. That doesn't have to be "complete freedom."

(B) is not necessary. The argument is not about everyone having equal access. Besides, nothing suggests that, in the past, everyone had equal access to public squares.

(D) is an Irrelevant Comparison. It doesn't matter what kind of discussion is more common. As long as the forum for important discussion exists, the author's argument stands. So, this is not necessary for the argument.

(E) is Out of Scope. Even if other types of public forums *do* exist, the author could still validly claim that the Internet should grant freedom of expression.

21. (C) Weaken

Step 1: Identify the Question Type

The correct answer will *undermine* the argument, which is a common LSAT term that means to weaken the argument.

Step 2: Untangle the Stimulus

Some children completed a program in which they learned to play chess. After the program was over, most of these children showed improvement in their schoolwork. The author concludes that their chess-playing skills contributed to their academic improvement.

Step 3: Make a Prediction

This is a classic case of Causation vs. Correlation. The students improved at school after the program, but were the chess skills (i.e., reasoning power and spatial intuition) really the *cause* of that improvement? The author assumes so, overlooking other possible causes. The correct answer will likely suggest that students improved in school for some other reason.

Step 4: Evaluate the Answer Choices

(C) offers an alternative explanation. If the chess team requires a high grade average, then students may have just wanted to join the team and were motivated to work harder. That suggests the higher performance was due to hard work, not necessarily the particular skills they learned in the chess program.

(A) is Out of Scope. Where other kids learn chess has no bearing on what made this particular group improve at school.

(B) is an Irrelevant Comparison. How these students compare to others before the program has no bearing on what caused their performance to improve. Even if they were high-performing kids to begin with, it's still possible the chess skills made them even better.

(D) is Out of Scope. The argument is not about reaching the *highest* level of achievement. Even if more effective solutions exist (e.g., study sessions), the chess skills could still provide *some* contribution to improved school performance.

(E) is an Irrelevant Comparison. The argument is about what led to improved school performance, not which students are better chess players.

22. (A) Parallel Reasoning

Step 1: Identify the Question Type

The question asks for an argument that is *similar* in its reasoning to the given argument. That makes this a Parallel Reasoning question.

Step 2: Untangle the Stimulus

On Wednesdays, Kate usually buys guava juice, which she can only get at the health food store. So, the author concludes she must go to the health food store some Wednesdays.

Evidence:

| If | Wednesday | → | usually buys guava juice | → | at health food store |

Conclusion: *Some Wednesdays Kate shops at the health food store.*

Step 3: Make a Prediction

This argument is logically sound. The correct answer will follow the same general format: on a particular occasion (Wednesdays), an event usually happens (Kate buys guava juice) that can only happen under certain circumstances (at the health food store). So, the author concludes that the circumstances must occur sometimes on the given occasion.

Step 4: Evaluate the Answer Choices

(A) is a match. On a particular occasion (dinner at Cafe Delice), an event usually happens (food prepared in the institute's kitchen) that can only happen under certain circumstances (by institute teachers). So, the author concludes that the circumstances must occur sometimes on the given occasion.

Evidence:

| If | CD dinner | → | usually prepared in main kitchen | → | by CI teachers |

Conclusion: *Some CD dinners are prepared by CI teachers.*

(B) is Extreme. The original argument is about what *usually* happens and what *sometimes* occurs. This argument is about "all dinners" and what *must* occur.

(C) does provide an event that usually happens (preparing food in the kitchen), but does not say it can *only* happen under certain circumstances. It just says that all teachers are *allowed* to use that kitchen. That allows other people to use it, too, so the conclusion is not as sound.

(D) is a Distortion. Most teachers *can* use the kitchen, but that doesn't mean they usually *do*. This also allows other people to use the kitchen, which makes the conclusion less sound.

(E) is a Distortion. Like the original, there's a particular occasion (dinner at Cafe Delice) on which an event usually happens (institute teachers prepare the meal). However, that event does not *have* to happen at the institute kitchen. The teachers are the only ones who can cook there, but they can just as likely cook elsewhere. This argument does not match.

23. (D) Weaken

Step 1: Identify the Question Type

The question is direct and asks for something that weakens the given argument.

Step 2: Untangle the Stimulus

The city is looking to switch from picking up recycling biweekly to weekly. The city claims this is more cost-effective because more recyclables collected means more revenue for the city. The editor argues otherwise, suggesting that the city won't really be collecting more recyclables.

Step 3: Make a Prediction

The argument is predicting what will happen under the new program, and predictions always hinge on the same assumption: relevant circumstances will go unchanged. In this case, the editor assumes that people will continue to put out an equal amount of recyclables under the new program. If the editor is overlooking a possible change that would cause people to put out *more* recyclables, then the argument is weakened.

Step 4: Evaluate the Answer Choices

(D) suggests a significant change. The new program will be easier to follow, and people will be more likely to put out their recyclables. That would allow for more recyclables to be collected, contrary to the editor's claims.

(A) is an Irrelevant Comparison, if not a 180. The cost of recycling compared to general trash collection has no bearing on the argument. Besides, this suggests that nothing is going to change, which is consistent with the editor's assumption.

(B) is an irrelevant hypothetical. It doesn't matter what would happen if more recyclables *were* collected. The argument is about whether the new plan would lead to such an increase or not.

(C) is irrelevant. The city's argument, as well as the editor's, is based entirely on *how much* is collected, not how long it takes to collect it.

(E) is a 180. Contractor fees do not affect how much recycling people will do. But, if contractors *did* raise fees, that would likely raise costs and give the editor another reason to dispute the city's program.

24. (D) Assumption (Necessary)

Step 1: Identify the Question Type

The question asks for an *assumption* that the argument *requires*, making this a Necessary Assumption question.

Step 2: Untangle the Stimulus

Some science courses are intended to be so difficult that only the most committed students pass them. However, the professor notes that the least enthusiastic students are passing the course. Hence, the professor concludes that these courses are not doing what they intend.

Step 3: Make a Prediction

The courses are meant to ensure that only the most committed students pass. To conclude that these courses are failing their purpose, the professor must believe some *less* committed students are passing. However, the evidence only mentions passing students that are least *enthusiastic*—a Mismatched Concept. The professor must assume that these least enthusiastic students are less committed to majoring in science.

Step 4: Evaluate the Answer Choices

(D) must be true, connecting the lack of enthusiasm with the lack of commitment. If this *weren't* true, and unenthusiastic students could nonetheless be highly committed, then the courses might be serving their purpose after all.

(A) is a Distortion. The only purpose mentioned for the courses is to pass committed students. This answer still does not make the needed connection between enthusiasm and commitment.

(B) is Out of Scope. The professor is not arguing whether science departments *should* (let alone "need to") weed out those that are not the most committed. The argument is merely about whether such programs are working.

(C) is a 180 at worst. This makes it so that the programs are weeding out the least *and* some of the most enthusiastic students. In that case, enthusiasm becomes irrelevant, and the professor has no argument as to whether the programs are properly targeting *committed* students.

(E) is Out of Scope. The professor never gives any indication whether courses *should* be designed this way. The argument is solely about whether they *work*.

25. (C) Paradox

Step 1: Identify the Question Type

The question asks for something that will *resolve* a discrepancy, making this a Paradox question.

Step 2: Untangle the Stimulus

To warn predators, birds and reptiles create hissing sounds so similar that the author suggests that the sounds first developed in a common ancestor. However, the common ancestors would have had predators that couldn't hear those sounds.

Step 3: Make a Prediction

Paradox questions come down to a question of "why." In this case, why would these warning sounds develop in a creature whose predators couldn't hear it? The ancestor must have found these sounds effective against predators somehow, and the correct answer should suggest how.

Step 4: Evaluate the Answer Choices

(C) resolves the issue. Even though the predators couldn't *hear* the sound, they could *see* the physical effect of producing the sound, which explains why the ancestor developed the sound in the first place.

(A) is a 180. If the predators *and* the ancestor itself couldn't hear the sound, then it's even more inexplicable why this sound developed in the first place.

(B) doesn't help. If the common ancestor had various techniques to threaten predators, it would make sense for modern birds and reptiles to use *those* as well. But this still doesn't explain the hissing sounds, which would have gone unheard by predators.

(D) is an Irrelevant Comparison. Even if hissing required little energy, the predators still couldn't hear it. Thus, the question remains why those sounds would be used at all if they had no effect on predators.

(E) is Out of Scope. The number of predators doesn't help explain why the ancestor would have developed a technique that couldn't be detected by whatever number of predators it had.

Logical Reasoning
Logical Reasoning Question Types

Argument-Based Questions

Main Point Question

A question that asks for an argument's conclusion or an author's main point. Typical question stems:

Which one the following most accurately expresses the conclusion of the argument as a whole?

Which one of the following sentences best expresses the main point of the scientist's argument?

Role of a Statement Question

A question that asks how a specific sentence, statement, or idea functions within an argument. Typical question stems:

Which one of the following most accurately describes the role played in the argument by the statement that automation within the steel industry allowed steel mills to produce more steel with fewer workers?

The claim that governmental transparency is a nation's primary defense against public-sector corruption figures in the argument in which one of the following ways?

Point at Issue Question

A question that asks you to identify the specific claim, statement, or recommendation about which two speakers/authors disagree (or, rarely, about which they agree). Typical question stems:

A point at issue between Tom and Jerry is

The dialogue most strongly supports the claim that Marilyn and Billy disagree with each other about which one of the following?

Method of Argument Question

A question that asks you to describe an author's argumentative strategy. In other words, the correct answer describes *how* the author argues (not necessarily what the author says). Typical question stems:

Which one of the following most accurately describes the technique of reasoning employed by the argument?

Julian's argument proceeds by

In the dialogue, Alexander responds to Abigail in which one of the following ways?

Parallel Reasoning Question

A question that asks you to identify the answer choice containing an argument that has the same logical structure and reaches the same type of conclusion as the argument in the stimulus does. Typical question stems:

The pattern of reasoning in which one of the following arguments is most parallel to that in the argument above?

The pattern of reasoning in which one of the following arguments is most similar to the pattern of reasoning in the argument above?

Assumption-Family Questions

Assumption Question

A question that asks you to identify one of the unstated premises in an author's argument. Assumption questions come in two varieties.

Necessary Assumption questions ask you to identify an unstated premise required for an argument's conclusion to follow logically from its evidence. Typical question stems:

Which one of the following is an assumption on which the argument depends?

Which one of the following is an assumption that the argument requires in order for its conclusion to be properly drawn?

Sufficient Assumption questions ask you to identify an unstated premise sufficient to establish the argument's conclusion on the basis of its evidence. Typical question stems:

The conclusion follows logically if which one of the following is assumed?

Which one of the following, if assumed, enables the conclusion above to be properly inferred?

Strengthen/Weaken Question

A question that asks you to identify a fact that, if true, would make the argument's conclusion more likely (Strengthen) or less likely (Weaken) to follow from its evidence. Typical question stems:

Strengthen

Which one of the following, if true, most strengthens the argument above?

Which one the following, if true, most strongly supports the claim above?

Weaken

Which one of the following, if true, would most weaken the argument above?

Which one of the following, if true, most calls into question the claim above?

Flaw Question

A question that asks you to describe the reasoning error that the author has made in an argument. Typical question stems:

The argument's reasoning is most vulnerable to criticism on the grounds that the argument

Which of the following identifies a reasoning error in the argument?

The reasoning in the correspondent's argument is questionable because the argument

Parallel Flaw Question

A question that asks you to identify the argument that contains the same error(s) in reasoning that the argument in the stimulus contains. Typical question stems:

The pattern of flawed reasoning exhibited by the argument above is most similar to that exhibited in which one of the following?

Which one of the following most closely parallels the questionable reasoning cited above?

Evaluate the Argument Question

A question that asks you to identify an issue or consideration relevant to the validity of an argument. Think of Evaluate questions as "Strengthen or Weaken" questions. The correct answer, if true, will strengthen the argument, and if false, will weaken the argument, or vice versa. Evaluate questions are very rare. Typical question stems:

Which one of the following would be most useful to know in order to evaluate the legitimacy of the professor's argument?

It would be most important to determine which one of the following in evaluating the argument?

Non-Argument Questions

Inference Question

A question that asks you to identify a statement that follows from the statements in the stimulus. It is very important to note the characteristics of the one correct and the four incorrect answers before evaluating the choices in Inference questions. Depending on the wording of the question stem, the correct answer to an Inference question may be the one that

- *must be true* if the statements in the stimulus are true

- is *most strongly supported* by the statements in the stimulus

- *must be false* if the statements in the stimulus are true

Typical question stems:

If all of the statements above are true, then which one of the following must also be true?

Which one of the following can be properly inferred from the information above?

If the statements above are true, then each of the following could be true EXCEPT:

Which one of the following is most strongly supported by the information above?

The statements above, if true, most support which one of the following?

The facts described above provide the strongest evidence against which one of the following?

Paradox Question

A question that asks you to identify a fact that, if true, most helps to explain, resolve, or reconcile an apparent contradiction. Typical question stems:

Which one of the following, if true, most helps to explain how both studies' findings could be accurate?

Which one the following, if true, most helps to resolve the apparent conflict in the spokesperson's statements?

Each one of the following, if true, would contribute to an explanation of the apparent discrepancy in the information above EXCEPT:

Principle Questions

Principle Question

A question that asks you to identify corresponding cases and principles. Some Principle questions provide a principle in the stimulus and call for the answer choice describing a case that corresponds to the principle. Others provide a specific case in the stimulus and call for the answer containing a principle to which that case corresponds.

On the LSAT, Principle questions almost always mirror the skills rewarded by other Logical Reasoning question types. After each of the following Principle question stems, we note the question type it resembles. Typical question stems:

Which one of the following principles, if valid, most helps to justify the reasoning above? (**Strengthen**)

Which one of the following most accurately expresses the principle underlying the reasoning above? (**Assumption**)

The situation described above most closely conforms to which of the following generalizations? (**Inference**)

Which one of the following situations conforms most closely to the principle described above? (**Inference**)

Which one of the following principles, if valid, most helps to reconcile the apparent conflict among the prosecutor's claims? (**Paradox**)

Parallel Principle Question

A question that asks you to identify a specific case that illustrates the same principle that is illustrated by the case described in the stimulus. Typical question stem:

Of the following, which one illustrates a principle that is most similar to the principle illustrated by the passage?

Untangling the Stimulus

Conclusion Types

The conclusions in arguments found in the Logical Reasoning section of the LSAT tend to fall into one of six categories:

1) Value Judgment (an evaluative statement; e.g., Action X is unethical, or Y's recital was poorly sung)

2) "If"/Then (a conditional prediction, recommendation, or assertion; e.g., If X is true, then so is Y, or If you an M, then you should do N)

3) Prediction (X *will* or *will not* happen in the future)

4) Comparison (X is taller/shorter/more common/less common, etc. than Y)

5) Assertion of Fact (X is true or X is false)

6) Recommendation (we *should* or *should not* do X)

One-Sentence Test

A tactic used to identify the author's conclusion in an argument. Consider which sentence in the argument is the one the author would keep if asked to get rid of everything except her main point.

Subsidiary Conclusion

A conclusion following from one piece of evidence and then used by the author to support his overall conclusion or main point. Consider the following argument:

> The pharmaceutical company's new experimental treatment did not succeed in clinical trials. As a result, the new treatment will not reach the market this year. Thus, the company will fall short of its revenue forecasts for the year.

Here, the sentence "As a result, the new treatment will not reach the market this year" is a subsidiary conclusion. It follows from the evidence that the new treatment failed in clinical trials, and it provides evidence for the overall conclusion that the company will not meet its revenue projections.

Keyword(s) in Logical Reasoning

A word or phrase that helps you untangle a question's stimulus by indicating the logical structure of the argument or the author's point. Here are three categories of Keywords to which LSAT experts pay special attention in Logical Reasoning:

Conclusion words; e.g., *therefore, thus, so, as a result, it follows that, consequently*, [evidence] *is evidence that* [conclusion]

Evidence word; e.g, *because, since, after all, for*, [evidence] *is evidence that* [conclusion]

Contrast words; e.g., *but, however, while, despite, in spite of, on the other hand* (These are especially useful in Paradox and Inference questions.)

Experts use Keywords even more extensively in Reading Comprehension. Learn the Keywords associated with the Reading Comprehension section, and apply them to Logical Reasoning when they are helpful.

Mismatched Concepts

One of two patterns to which authors' assumptions conform in LSAT arguments. Mismatched Concepts describes the assumption in arguments in which terms or concepts in the conclusion are different *in kind* from those in the evidence. The author assumes that there is a logical relationship between the different terms. For example:

> Bobby is a **championship swimmer**. Therefore, he **trains every day**.

Here, the words "trains every day" appear only in the conclusion, and the words "championship swimmer" appear only in the evidence. For the author to reach this conclusion from this evidence, he assumes that championship swimmers train every day.

Another example:

> Susan does **not eat her vegetables**. Thus, she will **not grow big and strong**.

In this argument, not growing big and strong is found only in the conclusion while not eating vegetables is found only in the evidence. For the author to reach this conclusion from this evidence, she must assume that eating one's vegetables is necessary for one to grow big and strong.

See also Overlooked Possibilities.

Overlooked Possibilities

One of two patterns to which authors' assumptions conform in LSAT arguments. Mismatched Concepts describes the assumption in arguments in which terms or concepts in the conclusion are different *in degree, scale, or level of certainty* from those in the evidence. The author assumes that there is no factor or explanation for the conclusion other than the one(s) offered in the evidence. For example:

> Samson does not have a ticket stub for this movie showing. Thus, Samson must have sneaked into the movie without paying.

The author assumes that there is no other explanation for Samson's lack of a ticket stub. The author overlooks several possibilities: e.g., Samson had a special pass for this showing of the movie; Samson dropped his ticket stub by accident or threw it away after entering the theater; someone else in Samson's party has all of the party members' ticket stubs in her pocket or handbag.

Another example:

> Jonah's marketing plan will save the company money. Therefore, the company should adopt Jonah's plan.

Here, the author makes a recommendation based on one advantage. The author assumes that the advantage is the company's only concern or that there are no disadvantages that could outweigh it, e.g., Jonah's plan might save money on marketing but not generate any new leads or customers; Jonah's plan might damage the company's image or reputation; Jonah's plan might include illegal false advertising. Whenever the author of an LSAT argument concludes with a recommendation or a prediction based on just a single fact in the evidence, that author is always overlooking many other possibilities.

See also Mismatched Concepts.

Causal Argument

An argument in which the author concludes or assumes that one thing causes another. The most common pattern on the LSAT is for the author to conclude that A causes B from evidence that A and B are correlated. For example:

> I notice that whenever the store has a poor sales month, employee tardiness is also higher that month. Therefore, it must be that employee tardiness causes the store to lose sales.

The author assumes that the correlation in the evidence indicates a causal relationship. These arguments are vulnerable to three types of overlooked possibilities:

1) There could be **another causal factor**. In the previous example, maybe the months in question are those in which the manager takes vacation, causing the store to lose sales and permitting employees to arrive late without fear of the boss's reprimands.

2) Causation could be **reversed**. Maybe in months when sales are down, employee morale suffers and tardiness increases as a result.

3) The correlation could be **coincidental**. Maybe the correlation between tardiness and the dip in sales is pure coincidence.

See also Flaw Types: Correlation versus Causation.

Another pattern in causal arguments (less frequent on the LSAT) involves the assumption that a particular causal mechanism is or is not involved in a causal relationship. For example:

> The airport has rerouted takeoffs and landings so that they will not create noise over the Sunnyside neighborhood. Thus, the recent drop in Sunnyside's property values cannot be explained by the neighborhood's proximity to the airport.

Here, the author assumes that the only way that the airport could be the cause of dropping property values is through noise pollution. The author overlooks any other possible mechanism (e.g., frequent traffic jams and congestion) through which proximity to the airport could be cause of Sunnyside's woes.

Principle

A broad, law-like rule, definition, or generalization that covers a variety of specific cases with defined attributes. To see how principles are treated on the LSAT, consider the following principle:

> It is immoral for a person for his own gain to mislead another person.

That principle would cover a specific case, such as a seller who lies about the quality of construction to get a higher price for his house. It would also correspond to the case of a teenager who, wishing to spend a night out on the town, tells his mom "I'm going over to Randy's house." He knows that his mom believes that he will be staying at Randy's house, when in fact, he and Randy will go out together.

That principle does not, however, cover cases in which someone lies solely for the purpose of making the other person feel better or in which one person inadvertently misleads the other through a mistake of fact.

Be careful not to apply your personal ethics or morals when analyzing the principles articulated on the test.

Flaw Types

Necessary versus Sufficient

This flaw occurs when a speaker or author concludes that one event is necessary for a second event from evidence that the first event is sufficient to bring about the second event, or vice versa. Example:

> If more than 25,000 users attempt to access the new app at the same time, the server will crash. Last night, at 11:15 pm, the server crashed, so it must be case that more than 25,000 users were attempting to use the new app at that time.

In making this argument, the author assumes that the only thing that will cause the server to crash is the usage level (i.e., high usage is *necessary* for the server to crash). The evidence, however, says that high usage is one thing that will cause the server to crash (i.e., that high usage is *sufficient* to crash the server).

Correlation versus Causation

This flaw occurs when a speaker or author draws a conclusion that one thing causes another from evidence that the two things are correlated. Example:

Over the past half century, global sugar consumption has tripled. That same time period has seen a surge in the rate of technological advancement worldwide. It follows that the increase in sugar consumption has caused the acceleration in technological advancement.

In any argument with this structure, the author is making three unwarranted assumptions. First, he assumes that there is no alternate cause, i.e., there is nothing else that has contributed to rapid technological advancement. Second, he assumes that the causation is not reversed, i.e., technological advancement has not contributed to the increase in sugar consumption, perhaps by making it easier to grow, refine, or transport sugar. And, third, he assumes that the two phenomena are not merely coincidental, i.e., that it is not just happenstance that global sugar consumption is up at the same time that the pace of technological advancement has accelerated.

Unrepresentative Sample

This flaw occurs when a speaker or author draws a conclusion about a group from evidence in which the sample cannot represent that group because the sample is too small or too selective, or is biased in some way. Example:

Moviegoers in our town prefer action films and romantic comedies over other film genres. Last Friday, we sent reporters to survey moviegoers at several theaters in town, and nearly 90 percent of those surveyed were going to watch either an action film or a romantic comedy.

The author assumes that the survey was representative of the town's moviegoers, but there are several reasons to question that assumption. First, we don't know how many people were actually surveyed. Even if the number of people surveyed was adequate, we don't know how many other types of movies were playing. Finally, the author doesn't limit her conclusion to moviegoers on Friday nights. If the survey had been conducted at Sunday matinees, maybe most moviegoers would have been heading out to see an animated family film or a historical drama. Who knows?

Scope Shift/Unwarranted Assumption

This flaw occurs when a speaker's or author's evidence has a scope or has terms different enough from the scope or terms in his conclusion that it is doubtful that the evidence can support the conclusion. Example:

A very small percentage of working adults in this country can correctly define collateralized debt obligation securities. Thus, sad to say, the majority of the nation's working adults cannot make prudent choices about how to invest their savings.

This speaker assumes that prudent investing requires the ability to accurately define a somewhat obscure financial term. But prudence is not the same thing as expertise, and

the speaker does not offer any evidence that this knowledge of this particular term is related to wise investing.

Percent versus Number/Rate versus Number

This flaw occurs when a speaker or author draws a conclusion about real quantities from evidence about rates or percentages, or vice versa. Example:

At the end of last season, Camp SunnyDay laid off half of their senior counselors and a quarter of their junior counselors. Thus, Camp SunnyDay must have more senior counselors than junior counselors.

The problem, of course, is that we don't know how many senior and junior counselors were on staff before the layoffs. If there were a total of 4 senior counselors and 20 junior counselors, then the camp would have laid off only 2 senior counselors while dismissing 5 junior counselors.

Equivocation

This flaw occurs when a speaker or author uses the same word in two different and incompatible ways. Example:

Our opponent in the race has accused our candidate's staff members of behaving unprofessionally. But that's not fair. Our staff is made up entirely of volunteers, not paid campaign workers.

The speaker interprets the opponent's use of the word *professional* to mean "paid," but the opponent likely meant something more along the lines of "mature, competent, and businesslike."

Ad Hominem

This flaw occurs when a speaker or author concludes that another person's claim or argument is invalid because that other person has a personal flaw or shortcoming. One common pattern is for the speaker or author to claim the other person acts hypocritically or that the other person's claim is made from self-interest. Example:

Mrs. Smithers testified before the city council, stating that the speed limits on the residential streets near her home are dangerously high. But why should we give her claim any credence? The way she eats and exercises, she's not even looking out for her own health.

The author attempts to undermine Mrs. Smithers's testimony by attacking her character and habits. He doesn't offer any evidence that is relevant to her claim about speed limits.

Part versus Whole

This flaw occurs when a speaker or author concludes that a part or individual has a certain characteristic because the whole or the larger group has that characteristic, or vice versa. Example:

Patient: I should have no problems taking the three drugs prescribed to me by my doctors. I looked them up, and none of the three is listed as having any major side effects.

Here, the patient is assuming that what is true of each of the drugs individually will be true of them when taken together. The patient's flaw is overlooking possible interactions that could cause problems not present when the drugs are taken separately.

Circular Reasoning

This flaw occurs when a speaker or author tries to prove a conclusion with evidence that is logically equivalent to the conclusion. Example:

> All those who run for office are prevaricators. To see this, just consider politicians: they all prevaricate.

Perhaps the author has tried to disguise the circular reasoning in this argument by exchanging the words "those who run for office" in the conclusion for "politicians" in the evidence, but all this argument amounts to is "Politicians prevaricate; therefore, politicians prevaricate." On the LSAT, circular reasoning is very rarely the correct answer to a Flaw question, although it is regularly described in one of the wrong answers.

Question Strategies

Denial Test

A tactic for identifying the assumption *necessary* to an argument. When you negate an assumption necessary to an argument, the argument will fall apart. Negating an assumption that is not necessary to the argument will not invalidate the argument. Consider the following argument:

> Only high schools which produced a state champion athlete during the school year will be represented at the Governor's awards banquet. Therefore, McMurtry High School will be represented at the Governor's awards banquet.

Which one of the following is an assumption necessary to that argument?

> (1) McMurtry High School produced more state champion athletes than any other high school during the school year.

> (2) McMurtry High School produced at least one state champion athlete during the school year.

If you are at all confused about which of those two statements reflects the *necessary* assumption, negate them both.

> (1) McMurtry High School **did not produce more** state champion athletes than any other high school during the school year.

That does not invalidate the argument. McMurtry could still be represented at the Governor's banquet.

> (2) McMurtry High School **did not produce any** state champion athletes during the school year.

Here, negating the statement causes the argument to fall apart. Statement (2) is an assumption *necessary* to the argument.

Point at Issue "Decision Tree"

A tactic for evaluating the answer choices in Point at Issue questions. The correct answer is the only answer choice to which you can answer "Yes" to all three questions in the following diagram.

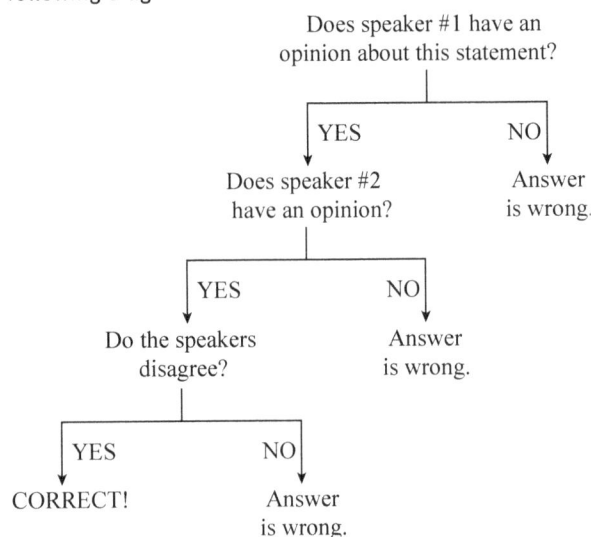

Common Methods of Argument

These methods of argument or argumentative strategies are common on the LSAT:

- Analogy, in which an author draws parallels between two unrelated (but purportedly similar) situations
- Example, in which an author cites a specific case or cases to justify a generalization
- Counterexample, in which an author seeks to discredit an opponent's argument by citing a specific case or cases that appear to invalidate the opponent's generalization
- Appeal to authority, in which an author cites an expert's claim or opinion as support for her conclusion
- Ad hominem attack, in which an author attacks her opponent's personal credibility rather than attacking the substance of her opponent's argument
- Elimination of alternatives, in which an author lists possibilities and discredits or rules out all but one

- Means/requirements, in which the author argues that something is needed to achieve a desired result

Wrong Answer Types in LR

Outside the Scope (Out of Scope; Beyond the Scope)

An answer choice containing a statement that is too broad, too narrow, or beyond the purview of the stimulus, making the statement in the choice irrelevant

180

An answer choice that directly contradicts what the correct answer must say (for example, a choice that strengthens the argument in a Weaken question)

Extreme

An answer choice containing language too emphatic to be supported by the stimulus; often (although not always) characterized by words such as *all*, *never*, *every*, *only*, or *most*

Distortion

An answer choice that mentions details from the stimulus but mangles or misstates what the author said about those details

Irrelevant Comparison

An answer choice that compares two items or attributes in a way not germane to the author's argument or statements

Half-Right/Half-Wrong

An answer choice that begins correctly, but then contradicts or distorts the passage in its second part; this wrong answer type is more common in Reading Comprehension than it is in Logical Reasoning

Faulty Use of Detail

An answer choice that accurately states something from the stimulus, but does so in a manner that answers the question incorrectly; this wrong answer type is more common in Reading Comprehension than it is in Logical Reasoning

Logic Games

Game Types

Strict Sequencing Game

A game that asks you to arrange entities into numbered positions or into a set schedule (usually hours or days). Strict Sequencing is, by far, the most common game type on the LSAT. In the typical Strict Sequencing game, there is a one-to-one matchup of entities and positions, e.g., seven entities to be placed in seven positions, one per position, or six entities to be placed over six consecutive days, one entity per day.

From time to time, the LSAT will offer Strict Sequencing with more entities than positions (e.g., seven entities to be arranged over five days, with some days to receive more than one entity) or more positions than entities (e.g., six entities to be scheduled over seven days, with at least one day to receive no entities).

Other, less common variations on Strict Sequencing include:

Double Sequencing, in which each entity is placed or scheduled two times (there have been rare occurrences of Triple or Quadruple Sequencing). Alternatively, a Double Sequencing game may involve two different sets of entities each sequenced once.

Circular Sequencing, in which entities are arranged around a table or in a circular arrangement (NOTE: When the positions in a Circular Sequencing game are numbered, the first and last positions are adjacent.)

Vertical Sequencing, in which the positions are numbered from top to bottom or from bottom to top (as in the floors of a building)

Loose Sequencing Game

A game that asks you to arrange or schedule entities in order but provides no numbering or naming of the positions. The rules in Loose Sequencing give only the relative positions (earlier or later, higher or lower) between two entities or among three entities. Loose Sequencing games almost always provide that there will be no ties between entities in the rank, order, or position they take.

Circular Sequencing Game

See Strict Sequencing Game.

Selection Game

A game that asks you to choose or include some entities from the initial list of entities and to reject or exclude others. Some Selection games provide overall limitations on the number of entities to be selected (e.g., "choose exactly four of seven students" or "choose at least two of six entrees") while others provide little or no restriction on the number selected ("choose at least one type of flower" or "select from among seven board members").

Distribution Game

A game that asks you to break up the initial list of entities into two, three, or (very rarely) four groups or teams. In the vast majority of Distribution games, each entity is assigned to one and only one group or team. A relatively common variation on Distribution games will provide a subdivided list of entities (e.g., eight students—four men and four women—will form three study groups) and will then require representatives from those subdivisions on each team (e.g., each study group will have at least one of the men on it).

Matching Game

A game that asks you to match one or more members of one set of entities to specific members of another set of entities, or that asks you to match attributes or objects to a set of entities. Unlike Distribution games, in which each entity is placed in exactly one group or team, Matching games usually permit you to assign the same attribute or object to more than one entity.

In some cases, there are overall limitations on the number of entities that can be matched (e.g., "In a school's wood shop, there are four workstations—numbered 1 through 4—and each workstation has at least one and at most three of the following tools—band saw, dremmel tool, electric sander, and power drill"). In almost all Matching games, further restrictions on the number of entities that can be matched to a particular person or place will be found in the rules (e.g., Workstation 4 will have more tools than Workstation 2 has).

Hybrid Game

A game that asks you to do two (or rarely, three) of the standard actions (Sequencing, Selection, Distribution, and Matching) to a set of entities.

The most common Hybrid is Sequencing-Matching. A typical Sequencing-Matching Hybrid game might ask you to schedule six speakers at a conference to six one-hour speaking slots (from 9 am to 2 pm), and then assign each speaker one of two subjects (economic development or trade policy).

Nearly as common as Sequencing-Matching is Distribution-Sequencing. A typical game of this type might ask you to divide six people in a talent competition into either a Dance category or a Singing category, and then rank the competitors in each category.

It is most common to see one Hybrid game in each Logic Games section, although there have been tests with two Hybrid games and tests with none. To determine the type of Hybrid you are faced with, identify the game's action in Step 1 of the Logic Games Method. For example, a game asking you to choose four of six runners, and then assign the four chosen runners to lanes numbered 1 through 4 on a track, would be a Selection-Sequencing Hybrid game.

Mapping Game

A game that provides you with a description of geographical locations and, typically, of the connections among them. Mapping games often ask you to determine the shortest possible routes between two locations or to account for the number of connections required to travel from one location to another. This game type is extremely rare, and as of February 2017, a Mapping game was last seen on PrepTest 40 administered in June 2003.

Process Game

A game that opens with an initial arrangement of entities (e.g., a starting sequence or grouping) and provides rules that describe the processes through which that arrangement can be altered. The questions typically ask you for acceptable arrangements or placements of particular entities after one, two, or three stages in the process. Occasionally, a Process game question might provide information about the arrangement after one, two, or three stages in the process and ask you what must have happened in the earlier stages. This game type is extremely rare, and as of November 2016, a Process game was last seen on PrepTest 16 administered in September 1995. However, there was a Process game on PrepTest 80, administered in December 2016, thus ending a 20-year hiatus.

Game Setups and Deductions

Floater

An entity that is not restricted by any rule or limitation in the game

Blocks of Entities

Two or more entities that are required by rule to be adjacent or separated by a set number of spaces (Sequencing games), to be placed together in the same group (Distribution games), to be matched to the same entity (Matching games), or to be selected or rejected together (Selection games)

Limited Options

Rules or restrictions that force all of a game's acceptable arrangements into two (or occasionally three) patterns

Established Entities

An entity required by rule to be placed in one space or assigned to one particular group throughout the entire game

Number Restrictions

Rules or limitations affecting the number of entities that may be placed into a group or space throughout the game

Duplications

Two or more rules that restrict a common entity. Usually, these rules can be combined to reach additional deductions. For example, if you know that B is placed earlier than A in a sequence and that C is placed earlier than B in that sequence, you can deduce that C is placed earlier than A in the sequence and that there is at least one space (the space occupied by B) between C and A.

Master Sketch

The final sketch derived from the game's setup, rules, and deductions. LSAT experts preserve the Master Sketch for reference as they work through the questions. The Master

Sketch does not include any conditions from New-"If" question stems.

Logic Games Question Types

Acceptability Question

A question in which the correct answer is an acceptable arrangement of all the entities relative to the spaces, groups, or selection criteria in the game. Answer these by using the rules to eliminate answer choices that violate the rules.

Partial Acceptability Question

A question in which the correct answer is an acceptable arrangement of some of the entities relative to some of the spaces, groups, or selection criteria in the game, and in which the arrangement of entities not included in the answer choices could be acceptable to the spaces, groups, or selection criteria not explicitly shown in the answer choices. Answer these the same way you would answer Acceptability questions, by using the rules to eliminate answer choices that explicitly or implicitly violate the rules.

Must Be True/False; Could Be True/False Question

A question in which the correct answer must be true, could be true, could be false, or must be false (depending on the question stem), and in which no additional rules or conditions are provided by the question stem

New-"If" Question

A question in which the stem provides an additional rule, condition, or restriction (applicable only to that question), and then asks what must/could be true/false as a result. LSAT experts typically handle New-"If" questions by copying the Master Sketch, adding the new restriction to the copy, and working out any additional deductions available as a result of the new restriction before evaluating the answer choices.

Rule Substitution Question

A question in which the correct answer is a rule that would have an impact identical to one of the game's original rules on the entities in the game

Rule Change Question

A question in which the stem alters one of the original rules in the game, and then asks what must/could be true/false as a result. LSAT experts typically handle Rule Change questions by reconstructing the game's sketch, but now accounting for the changed rule in place of the original. These questions are rare on recent tests.

Rule Suspension Question

A question in which the stem indicates that you should ignore one of the original rules in the game, and then asks what must/could be true/false as a result. LSAT experts typically handle Rule Suspension questions by reconstructing

the game's sketch, but now accounting for the absent rule. These questions are very rare.

Complete and Accurate List Question

A question in which the correct answer is a list of any and all entities that could acceptably appear in a particular space or group, or a list of any and all spaces or groups in which a particular entity could appear

Completely Determine Question

A question in which the correct answer is a condition that would result in exactly one acceptable arrangement for all of the entities in the game

Supply the "If" Question

A question in which the correct answer is a condition that would guarantee a particular result stipulated in the question stem

Minimum/Maximum Question

A question in which the correct answer is the number corresponding to the fewest or greatest number of entities that could be selected (Selection), placed into a particular group (Distribution), or matched to a particular entity (Matching). Often, Minimum/Maximum questions begin with New-"If" conditions.

Earliest/Latest Question

A question in which the correct answer is the earliest or latest position in which an entity may acceptably be placed. Often, Earliest/Latest questions begin with New-"If" conditions.

"How Many" Question

A question in which the correct answer is the exact number of entities that may acceptably be placed into a particular group or space. Often, "How Many" questions begin with New-"If" conditions.

Reading Comprehension
Strategic Reading

Roadmap

The test taker's markup of the passage text in Step 1 (Read the Passage Strategically) of the Reading Comprehension Method. To create helpful Roadmaps, LSAT experts circle or underline Keywords in the passage text and jot down brief, helpful notes or paragraph summaries in the margin of their test booklets.

Keyword(s) in Reading Comprehension

Words in the passage text that reveal the passage structure or the author's point of view and thus help test takers anticipate and research the questions that accompany the passage. LSAT experts pay attention to six categories of Keywords in Reading Comprehension:

Emphasis/Opinion—words that signal that the author finds a detail noteworthy or that the author has positive or negative opinion about a detail; any subjective or evaluative language on the author's part (e.g., *especially*, *crucial*, *unfortunately*, *disappointing*, *I suggest*, *it seems likely*)

Contrast—words indicating that the author finds two details or ideas incompatible or that the two details illustrate conflicting points (e.g., *but*, *yet*, *despite*, *on the other hand*)

Logic—words that indicate an argument, either the author's or someone else's (e.g., *thus*, *therefore*, *because*, *it follows that*)

Illustration—words indicating an example offered to clarify or support another point (e.g., *for example*, *this shows*, *to illustrate*)

Sequence/Chronology—words showing steps in a process or developments over time (e.g., *traditionally*, *in the past*, *today*, *first*, *second*, *finally*, *earlier*, *subsequent*)

Continuation—words indicating that a subsequent example or detail supports the same point or illustrates the same idea as the previous example (e.g., *moreover*, *in addition*, *also*, *further*, *along the same lines*)

Margin Notes

The brief notes or paragraph summaries that the test taker jots down next to the passage in the margin of the test booklet

Big Picture Summaries: Topic/Scope/Purpose/Main Idea

A test taker's mental summary of the passage as a whole made during Step 1 (Read the Passage Strategically) of the Reading Comprehension Method. LSAT experts account for four aspects of the passage in their big picture summaries:

Topic—the overall subject of the passage

Scope—the particular aspect of the Topic that the author focuses on

Purpose—the author's reason or motive for writing the passage (express this as a verb; e.g., *to refute*, *to outline*, *to evaluate*, *to critique*)

Main Idea—the author's conclusion or overall takeaway; if the passage does not contain an explicit conclusion or thesis, you can combine the author's Scope and Purpose to get a good sense of the Main Idea.

Passage Types

Kaplan categorizes Reading Comprehension passages in two ways, by subject matter and by passage structure.

Subject matter categories

In the majority of LSAT Reading Comprehension sections, there is one passage from each of the following subject matter categories:

Humanities—topics from art, music, literature, philosophy, etc.

Natural Science—topics from biology, astronomy, paleontology, physics, etc.

Social Science—topics from anthropology, history, sociology, psychology, etc.

Law—topics from constitutional law, international law, legal education, jurisprudence, etc.

Passage structure categories

The majority of LSAT Reading Comprehension passages correspond to one of the following descriptions. The first categories—Theory/Perspective and Event/Phenomenon—have been the most common on recent LSATs.

Theory/Perspective—The passage focuses on a thinker's theory or perspective on some aspect of the Topic; typically (though not always), the author disagrees and critiques the thinker's perspective and/or defends his own perspective.

Event/Phenomenon—The passage focuses on an event, a breakthrough development, or a problem that has recently arisen; when a solution to the problem is proposed, the author most often agrees with the solution (and that represents the passage's Main Idea).

Biography—The passage discusses something about a notable person; the aspect of the person's life emphasized by the author reflects the Scope of the passage.

Debate—The passage outlines two opposing positions (neither of which is the author's) on some aspect of the Topic; the author may side with one of the positions, may remain neutral, or may critique both. (This structure has been relatively rare on recent LSATs.)

Comparative Reading

A pair of passages (labeled Passage A and Passage B) that stand in place of the typical single passage exactly one time in each Reading Comprehension section administered since June 2007. The paired Comparative Reading passages share the same Topic, but may have different Scopes and Purposes. On most LSAT tests, a majority of the questions accompanying Comparative Reading passages require the test taker to compare or contrast ideas or details from both passages.

Question Strategies

Research Clues

A reference in a Reading Comprehension question stem to a word, phrase, or detail in the passage text, or to a particular line number or paragraph in the passage. LSAT experts recognize five kinds of research clues:

Line Reference—An LSAT expert researches around the referenced lines, looking for Keywords that indicate why the referenced details were included or how they were used by the author.

Paragraph Reference—An LSAT expert consults her passage Roadmap to see the paragraph's Scope and Purpose.

Quoted Text (often accompanied by a line reference)—An LSAT expert checks the context of the quoted term or phrase, asking what the author meant by it in the passage.

Proper Nouns—An LSAT expert checks the context of the person, place, or thing in the passage, asking whether the author made a positive, negative, or neutral evaluation of it and why the author included it in the passage.

Content Clues—These are terms, concepts, or ideas from the passage mentioned in the question stem but not as direct quotes and not accompanied by line references. An LSAT expert knows that content clues almost always refer to something that the author emphasized or about which the author expressed an opinion.

Reading Comp Question Types

Global Question

A question that asks for the Main Idea of the passage or for the author's primary Purpose in writing the passage. Typical question stems:

> Which one of the following most accurately expresses the main point of the passage?

> The primary purpose of the passage is to

Detail Question

A question that asks what the passage explicitly states about a detail. Typical question stems:

> According to the passage, some critics have criticized Gilliam's films on the grounds that

> The passage states that one role of a municipality's comptroller in budget decisions by the city council is to

> The author identifies which one of the following as a commonly held but false preconception?

> The passage contains sufficient information to answer which of the following questions?

Occasionally, the test will ask for a correct answer that contains a detail *not* stated in the passage:

> The author attributes each of the following positions to the Federalists EXCEPT:

Inference Question

A question that asks for a statement that follows from or is based on the passage but that is not necessarily stated explicitly in the passage. Some Inference questions contain research clues. The following are typical Inference question stems containing research clues:

> Based on the passage, the author would be most likely to agree with which one of the following statements about unified field theory?

> The passage suggests which one of the following about the behavior of migratory water fowl?

> Given the information in the passage, to which one of the following would radiocarbon dating techniques likely be applicable?

Other Inference questions lack research clues in the question stem. They may be evaluated using the test taker's Big Picture Summaries, or the answer choices may make it clear that the test taker should research a particular part of the passage text. The following are typical Inference question stems containing research clues:

> It can be inferred from the passage that the author would be most likely to agree that

> Which one of the following statements is most strongly supported by the passage?

Other Reading Comprehension question types categorized as Inference questions are Author's Attitude questions and Vocabulary-in-Context questions.

Logic Function Question

A question that asks why the author included a particular detail or reference in the passage or how the author used a particular detail or reference. Typical question stems:

> The author of the passage mentions declining inner-city populations in the paragraph most likely in order to

> The author's discussion of Rimbaud's travels in the Mediterranean (lines 23–28) functions primarily to

> Which one of the following best expresses the function of the third paragraph in the passage?

Logic Reasoning Question

A question that asks the test taker to apply Logical Reasoning skills in relation to a Reading Comprehension passage. Logic Reasoning questions often mirror Strengthen or Parallel Reasoning questions, and occasionally mirror Method of Argument or Principle questions. Typical question stems:

> Which one of the following, if true, would most strengthen the claim made by the author in the last sentence of the passage (lines 51–55)?

> Which one of the following pairs of proposals is most closely analogous to the pair of studies discussed in the passage?

Author's Attitude Question

A question that asks for the author's opinion or point of view on the subject discussed in the passage or on a detail mentioned in the passage. Since the correct answer may follow from the passage without being explicitly stated in it, some Author's Attitude questions are characterized as a subset of Inference questions. Typical question stems:

> The author's attitude toward the use of DNA evidence in the appeals by convicted felons is most accurately described as

> The author's stance regarding monetarist economic theories can most accurately be described as one of

Vocabulary-in-Context Question

A question that asks how the author uses a word or phrase within the context of the passage. The word or phrase in question is always one with multiple meanings. Since the correct answer follows from its use in the passage, Vocabulary-in-Context questions are characterized as a subset of Inference questions. Typical question stems:

> Which one of the following is closest in meaning to the word "citation" as it used in the second paragraph of the passage (line 18)?

> In context, the word "enlightenment" (line 24) refers to

Wrong Answer Types in RC

Outside the Scope (Out of Scope; Beyond the Scope)

An answer choice containing a statement that is too broad, too narrow, or beyond the purview of the passage

180

An answer choice that directly contradicts what the correct answer must say

Extreme

An answer choice containing language too emphatic (e.g., *all*, *never*, *every*, *none*) to be supported by the passage

Distortion

An answer choice that mentions details or ideas from the passage but mangles or misstates what the author said about those details or ideas

Faulty Use of Detail

An answer choice that accurately states something from the passage but in a manner that incorrectly answers the question

Half-Right/Half-Wrong

An answer choice in which one clause follows from the passage while another clause contradicts or deviates from the passage

Formal Logic Terms

Conditional Statement ("If"-Then Statement)

A statement containing a sufficient clause and a necessary clause. Conditional statements can be described in Formal Logic shorthand as:

> If [sufficient clause]   → [necessary clause]

In some explanations, the LSAT expert may refer to the sufficient clause as the statement's "trigger" and to the necessary clause as the statement's result.

For more on how to interpret, describe, and use conditional statements on the LSAT, please refer to "A Note About Formal Logic on the LSAT" in this book's introduction.

Contrapositive

The conditional statement logically equivalent to another conditional statement formed by reversing the order of and negating the terms in the original conditional statement. For example, reversing and negating the terms in this statement:

> *If* A → B

results in its contrapositive:

> *If* $\sim B$ → $\sim A$

To form the contrapositive of conditional statements in which either the sufficient clause or the necessary clause has more than one term, you must also change the conjunction *and* to *or*, or vice versa. For example, reversing and negating the terms and changing *and* to *or* in this statement:

> *If* M → $O \ AND \ P$

results in its contrapositive:

> *If* $\sim O \ OR \sim P$ → $\sim M$

www.ingramcontent.com/pod-product-compliance
Lightning Source LLC
Chambersburg PA
CBHW081259040426
42452CB00014B/2575